WORTH IT

Dr. Simmons reminds Christian parents of their God-given responsibility to partner with God in raising up a godly generation through providing their children a biblical education, which is clearly explained in the book. He encourages parents that there is help through a unified message from the home, church, and Christian school. Interwoven through the book are powerful examples of a diversity of Christian schools, teachers, students, and parents from the Association of Christian Schools International family who have experienced and demonstrated the power of a truly Christian education. An insightful and encouraging read for every parent desiring to have his or her children challenged to see the entire universe from a biblical worldview!

—Dr. Charles Ware, President, Crossroads Bible College, Indianapolis, Indiana

Dr. Simmons' book, *Worth It*, beautifully presents the cause of Christian school education in a compelling reading style. Once I started reading it, I couldn't put it down. I heartily recommend it.

—Paul Kienel, ACSI President Emeritus

Dr. Brian Simmons writes with personal passion. Using biblical principles, real-life stories, and logic, he makes the case that Christian schools are a critical element in the discipleship of a young person's life while challenging common misunderstandings regarding Christian schools. *Worth It* draws parents to Christian schooling like a magnet and places life in perspective by focusing on what ultimately matters in the lives of our children—eternity!

—Jeffrey D. Wilcox, Superintendent, Heritage Christian School, Indianapolis, Indiana

Brian Simmons brings excellence to Christian education. He's been an incredible blessing to our work at Harvest Christian Academy. We appreciate his many efforts. As you read, learn from him, and your ministry will be better for it.

—Dr. James MacDonald, Senior Pastor, Harvest Bible Chapel

It is nice to see the case for Christian education written in a clear way that shows the benefits, the results, and the rewards of being involved in a local Christian school.

—Dan Stroup, Teacher, Heritage Christian School, Indianapolis, Indiana

Dr. Simmons has done an outstanding job of not only making the case for Christian schools but also addressing reasons that parents may have for not sending their children. His work is not only spiritually sound but also sprinkled with compelling, real-life examples of parents who have made this choice for their children and who give their reasons for doing so. This book is a very useful tool for pastors and administrators.

—Tim Greener, Superintendent, Christian Academy School System,
Louisville, Kentucky

This book makes a convincing case for Christian schooling. Clearly, the Lord is passionate for His children and for their distinctively Christian educational training. Christian families and the Christian Church would wisely align their passions with the Lord's. God is intimately and uniquely involved with Christian schools and their students.

—Todd R. Marrah, EdD, Superintendent, Tree of Life Christian Schools, Columbus, Ohio

Worth It is a must-read for every Christian parent and educator. Dr. Simmons combines a strong biblical foundation and real-life stories to make a case for providing our children with a Bible-based, Christ-centered education. If parents want their children to survive and thrive in today's anti-Christian culture, then they must pay attention to the challenging words presented here. And Christian school educators will find this resource a valuable self-examination tool to make sure that their schools are doing those things that will make an impact on lives for eternity.

—Glen Schultz, EdD, Headmaster, Sherwood Christian Academy, Albany, Georgia

Brian Simmons has provided a needed apologetic for the important role of Christian education for students, parents, and our society. This book is a helpful guide for those seeking to make the best decisions regarding the education of their children. Dr. Simmons covers the primary educational issues facing parents and composes a strong case for the investment in a Christ-centered educational experience.

—R. Scott Rodin, Managing Principal, The Not-for-Profit Practice of OneAccord, Bellevue, Washington

This is "easy reading with an unmoving purpose"—tremendous, meaningful, real-life illustrations of the impact of a Christ-centered education on families with kids from all walks of life, illustrations that use everything from Bible class to football to missions to creative arts to show the tremendous payback received for investing in the lives of the students in Christian schools around the world. This book needs to be read by everyone in the spectrum of Christian education!

—Bruce D. Johnson, Superintendent, Redwood Christian Schools, Castro Valley, California

Brian Simmons has dedicated his life and his career to advancing God's kingdom through Christian schooling. His passion comes through on every page of this wonderful apologetic for the cause of distinctively Christian education. This is not just another treatise on a Christian philosophy of education but rather a great collection of stories. Dr. Simmons' book should be required reading for Christian parents!

—Mickey Bowdon, Vice President for Christian School Education, Columbia International University, Columbia, South Carolina

WORTH IT

THE 15,000-HOUR DECISION

BRIAN S. SIMMONS
WITH STEVE RABEY

purposeful design®
publications

Colorado Springs, Colorado

Purposeful Design Publications is the publishing division of the Association of Christian Schools International (ACSI) and is committed to the ministry of Christian school education, to enable Christian educators and schools worldwide to effectively prepare students for life. As the publisher of textbooks, trade books, and other educational resources within ACSI, Purposeful Design Publications strives to produce biblically sound materials that reflect Christian scholarship and stewardship and that address the identified needs of Christian schools around the world.

Printed in the United States of America
20 19 18 17 16 15 14 13 12 11   1 2 3 4 5 6 7

Simmons, Brian S. with Steve Rabey
    Worth it: The 15,000-hour decision
    ISBN 978-1-58331-386-2 Catalog #6625

Designer: Bethany Kerstetter
Editorial team: Cheryl Chiapperino, Gina Brandon

Purposeful Design Publications
A Division of ACSI
PO Box 65130 • Colorado Springs CO 80962-5130
Customer Service: 800-367-0798 • www.acsi.org

DEDICATION

As I think back over the years of my life, I value more and more the guidance and direction of my father, Russell Eugene Simmons. From fishing on Saturdays to long games of chess, my dad demonstrated his love to me by spending time with me. Thanks, Dad, for impressing on my heart the true definition of success (Joshua 1:8). I am certain you now know, from the perspective of eternity, that your investment in my life was *Worth It*!

CONTENTS

FOREWORD

I am a raving fan of Christian education, so you can imagine my delight in being asked to write this foreword for Brian Simmons' book, which so clearly articulates the importance of a maximum educational experience for every generation.

The psalmist states that "[God's] truth endures to all generations" (Psalm 100:5, NKJV), and since Christian education partners with that promise, it is a highly valued enterprise.

There are few things more important than our children and our stewardship of their capacity to be effective successors as they follow the path that we have walked before them. The fact that God has entrusted them to our care is a sobering yet exciting assignment. We steward them on many fronts—health, safety, love, nurture, discipline, and education.

Christian education is by its very nature holistic, in that it cares for the totality of a student's development. Mind, spirit, and soul are all the priorities of a Christ-centered educational experience—to say nothing of the integration of the lordship of Christ into all the curricular offerings. To teach history without acknowledging the God of history and His sovereign, providential oversight of the affairs of all of humanity as He guides history to its climactic victory at the end of time is to shortchange a student's educational experience. The same could be said for the importance of the profound recognition that Christ is the creator and sustainer of the complex yet glorious systems of math, biology, and the sciences that hold the world together in a predictable and meaningful whole. Philosophy celebrates and stimulates the life of the mind for the glory of a God who is the ultimate source of wisdom and truth. Actually, in the end, all of education should lead us to worship the marvel and mystery of our transcendent and all-wise God.

Read this book carefully. And weigh the strategic potential of entrusting the coming generation's youth to an educational experience that maximizes their opportunity to go out into our world to engage the cultures of our world for Christ through their callings and careers.

—Dr. Joe Stowell, President, Cornerstone University,
Grand Rapids, Michigan

PREFACE

As a lifelong educator and administrator, I have seen many outstanding teachers at work. One of the techniques good teachers often use before they present their daily history or math lesson is to ask their students provocative questions to get the students' brains working.

That's the approach I would like to use with you as I start this book. Are you ready? Here are a few questions to get us started:

1. What do you think of when you hear the words *Christian school*?
2. What kinds of emotions and mental images do you have about Christian schools?
3. And what does the term *Christian education* mean to you?

As I ask adults these questions, I am surprised at the diversity of answers I receive. Some parents have mixed feelings about Christian schools. In some cases these feelings are based on personal experience. In other cases, they are based on conversations with other parents or educators, or on personal observations at church or in the community. Regardless of what adults may think about Christian schools, most of the Christian parents I have met care deeply about providing their kids with some form of Christian education as a foundation for life.

THE CASE FOR CHRISTIAN SCHOOLS

In following pages, I am going to make the case that parents who want to provide the highest-quality biblical foundation for their children should enroll them in a Christian school as soon as possible.

Of course, you would expect me to say something like this. As president of the Association of Christian Schools International (ACSI), I would probably surprise you if I said anything different.

But I'm not promoting Christian schools merely because it's my job to do so. I believe in Christian schools because I've seen the powerful results they have achieved in my own life, in the lives of my children, and in the lives of thousands of men and women who are making the world a better place by living out the commitments and using the skills that were developed in these former Christian school students through caring and professional Christian teachers.

I also have a unique advantage. As president of ACSI, I have been privileged to see the best-of-the-best Christian schooling worldwide. I take advantage of each chance I have to see a school I have never visited before. Time and again I witness the ways creative teachers plant the seed of God's Word in young hearts and minds. I come away from these visits even more convinced than ever before that parents who care about their children and want to provide the very best preparation possible for the future will entrust their children to the loving people who work in ACSI member schools—preschools, K–12 schools, and Christian colleges and universities near and far.

But don't take my word for it. Come along with me as we take a quick guided tour of what Christian schooling means to the parents and children who have experienced its transformative power firsthand.

There are more than twenty-two thousand ACSI member schools in our world. I would love to show each one of them to you, but that would be impossible. So I will discipline myself to highlight only a few.

No matter what you think about Christian schooling before you read this book, I hope you are open to having your mind expanded by the life-changing work that is going on in classrooms small and large, in remote towns and big cities, in the United States and more than one hundred countries around the world.

A CHRISTIAN SCHOOL FOR YOU AND YOUR KIDS?

Since you picked up this book, there's a good chance you're thinking about Christian schooling for your child; so let me share my thoughts with you as you consider whether a Christian school would be best for your uniquely fashioned son or daughter. These thoughts will provide a preview of some of the insights you will find in chapters 1–6 of this book.

HELPING STUDENTS DEVELOP

First, the Christian schools affiliated with ACSI are committed to *helping students achieve their full, God-given potential*. Each one of us is created as a unique child of God. The teachers and staff of Christian schools believe that their number one job is to help your children find that uniqueness, develop it, and use it throughout their lives for the glory of God. (See chapter 2 for more about schools that encourage students to glorify God.)

CHRIST, THE FOCUS

Second, there's a *distinctive faith-based Christian dimension* to Christian schools. This may seem obvious, but I find that many parents believe that their children are adequately served by churches and public schools. But having been in and around Christian schools my entire life, I have seen the unique role these schools play in forming and strengthening the faith of their students. And this is something that secular schools, both public (including public charter) and private, are unable to provide.

You may have excellent churches as well as top-notch public and private schools in your community. Still, I believe that Christian schools, in partnership with the home and the church, are best equipped to prepare your children for living out their faith in our challenging and demanding world. (For more on this faith dimension, see chapter 2.)

WORLD-CLASS EDUCATION

Third, some parents are concerned that Christian schools may not be on par academically with other schools. While this may have been the case with some schools in some places, I am here to tell you that, overall, Christian schools provide students with *world-class learning* that compares to or even exceeds what's available at other schools. These stellar outcomes are the result of committed and well-trained teachers using the academic resources God provides. These godly educators serve as role models for students not only by providing effective instruction but also by maintaining consistent school discipline in a loving and caring environment.

Taken together, I believe that these factors make Christian schooling the best choice for the education of your kids. (See more on our commitment to academic excellence in Chapter 3.)

TEACHERS WHO CARE AND GET INVOLVED

Fourth, the teachers at Christian schools are committed to helping your children academically, emotionally, socially, and spiritually. I can't claim that our teachers are better people than teachers in other institutions. But what I can say is this: In Christian schools *teachers, who mentor and disciple students*, combine a concern for academics, for spiritual growth, and for involvement in all aspects of student life. But in public schools even the best and most concerned teachers are often prevented from sharing their faith and getting involved in the spiritual lives of students.

Parents entrust a large portion of their children's lives to schools. (See the chapter 1 sidebar, which discusses the "fifteen-thousand-hour question.") Don't you want to be assured that the teachers and staff at your kids' school care as much about serving Christ as you do? (See more about the concern of our teachers in chapter 4, "The Human Touch.")

YOUR BEST INVESTMENT IN YOUR CHILDREN'S LIVES

Fifth, I believe that Christian schools are a *worthwhile investment that keeps on giving* throughout your children's lives. We all know that it costs money for the privilege of sending your children to a private Christian school. In fact, in the United States and many countries of the world, parents must pay twice (taxes and tuition) to send their children to a private school. I believe that these costs, while not insignificant, are minimal when compared with the life-transforming opportunities and tangible spiritual growth that your children will experience at a Christian school. (See more about cost-benefit analyses in chapter 5.)

HOPE FOR THE FUTURE

Finally, I believe that Christian schools are *our hope for the future.* What do I mean by that? Let me explain. Our world is big and complex, and it is becoming more complex every day. Many sources have estimated that the world's population will pass the 7-billion mark in 2011. As we look at this ever-changing world, we see many needs: challenges to be addressed, problems to be solved, and ancient tensions to be healed.

I believe that the students in Christian schools (both around the world and in the United States) hold the key to addressing these pressing needs, because these students are best able to understand who people are, how the world works, and what God expects of them.

ACKNOWLEDGMENTS

The older I get, the more thankful I am for the abundant grace of God in my life. Thank you, Lord, for the gift of your Son, Jesus Christ. Thank you for loving parents, Gene and Loretta Simmons. Thank you for bringing my wife, Bonnie, and her precious family and especially my mother- and father-in-law, Elaine and Larry McCauley, into my life. I will never forget my first glimpse of Bonnie at Cornerstone University! And now, as we have passed the milestone of thirty years of marriage, our relationship grows sweeter by the day. Thank you, Lord, for my children, Jared, Drew, Lindi, and Aubrey. Thank you, too, for my daughter-in-law, Mary Claire. I realize that these relationships have been entrusted to my care for only a short time. Lord, help me to be a faithful steward. With a grateful heart, I meditate on these words often: "But be sure to fear the Lord and faithfully serve him. Think of all the wonderful things he has done for you" (1 Samuel 12:24, NLT).

As I look back over this book project of the last two years, I want to thank Steve Babbitt, the assistant vice president of Purposeful Design, for his support, advice, and encouragement. Thanks also to my coauthor, Steve Rabey. This book would not have been possible without you! And thanks to the entire ACSI team and Executive Board for your faithfulness to the Lord and to the mission and vision of ACSI. A special thanks to Beth Elder for your wise counsel, support, and effective leadership as I transitioned to my current role. I count it a joy and a privilege to serve the Lord alongside each one of you.

Thanks to Paul Young, Mickey Bowdon, and my Christian School Roundtable friends. You all are a dear and constant source of prayer, advice, and encouragement for me.

When a student is fully grown, he will be like his teacher (Luke 6:40): Thank you to Barry Smith, Dave Rottman, Mike Reece, Peter Atwood, Ron Meyers, Ray "Gator" Gates, Ted Kowalski, and so many other teachers God used to shape my life. I carry a piece of you with me even now. Thanks to my pastor of eighteen years, Dan Gelatt, for caring enough to "meddle." Thanks to Bob and Polly Reese for following the Lord's leading in your lives and making Elkhart Christian Academy a reality. You built this school for me and for many others, and your investment was certainly worth the cost! Thanks to my first secretary, Ruth Curran, and to Pastor David Graham for our long morning walks.

I look back on my first few professional leadership experiences and remember lifetime friends like Phil Gelatt, Dwight Peterson, Sue Alberts, Al Leinbach, Mary Jane English, Brian Dougherty, Ron Qualls, Mary Lou Cooper, Jim Milligan, Bill Chapman, Mark Alt, Tom Abernethy, Mitch Morgan, Tim Craiger, Phil Byars, the "Be One" Sunday school class, and so many others. It has been said that a leader is three feet out in front of those he leads. If you are ten feet ahead, you are a target; and if you are a hundred feet ahead, you are a martyr. Thanks to each of you for walking by my side.

Thanks to President Henry Smith, his cabinet, the university relations team, my grad school colleagues, and my many dear friends at Indiana Wesleyan University. My family and I have been deeply blessed by all of you! Thanks to Paul Kienel, a founder and the president emeritus of ACSI, and his dear wife, Annie. You both are a constant source of love, encouragement, and support! And thanks to my executive assistant, Sandy Kenny, for keeping me on track.

My friend Walt Wiley says, "If a man thinketh he leadeth and hath no one following, he is only out for a walk." Thanks to my ACSI senior leadership team, Taylor Smith, Dan Egeler, Derek Keenan, Jere Elliott, Tom Cathey, Walt Tracy, and Sam Barfell, for your partnership in ministry.

Christian school education is a cause worth giving our lives to. To have a major part in making thoroughly prepared, sold-out, full-throttle disciples of Jesus Christ is definitely *Worth It*!

INTRODUCTION

AROUND THE WORLD IN TWENTY-TWO THOUSAND SCHOOLS

Around the world, dedicated Christian school teachers and leaders teach and train children for the work of God's kingdom. In fact, I believe Christian school education is the next tsunami in world evangelism and discipleship. If you're ready to see what an amazing thing Christian schooling is, buckle yourself in for a brief but whirlwind journey.

A SCHOOL ON THE SEA

We start our tour on board the Mercy Ships Academy, a floating school for about 50 students whose parents are serving on Mercy Ships, which circle the globe and provide much-needed medical care to impoverished people.

Founded in 1978 by the organization Youth with a Mission, Mercy Ships operate under this slogan: "Bringing hope and healing to the world's forgotten poor." The men and women who serve on the ship provide needed medical care to some of the most disadvantaged people on earth. And while the moms and the dads are providing care, the sons and the daughters attend classes in one of the most unique schools in the world.

Most ACSI member schools are on land though. So let me introduce you to some other schools that demonstrate the impact Christian schooling is having on our world.

CHRISTIANS AND MUSLIMS STUDYING TOGETHER IN AFRICA

One of the ACSI employees who travels the globe to serve our member schools is Dan Egeler, the senior vice president of ACSI Global. Dan has visited hundreds of schools in dozens of countries. One of the schools that has significantly impressed him is Hillcrest School, which serves some 280 students in Jos, Nigeria.

Jos is a bustling city of nearly a million people that has a history of violent tension between Christians and Muslims. In January 2010 two hundred people died in religious riots there. That's why it is so exciting to see what is happening at Hillcrest today: "The school is a point of light that proves Muslims and Christians can live together in harmony," says Dan. "Christian and Muslim kids have become best friends in the midst of one of the most intense conflicts in the continent of Africa."

The nearby Muslim families are so impressed by the quality of the schooling at Hillcrest that they enroll their own children, who are required to study the Bible and attend chapel services along with all the Christian students. Some of the Muslim students have accepted Christ, as have some of their family members. But even the students who remain Muslims experience a sense of love and respect that is rare in this divided city.

"This school is a 'city on a hill,'[1] " says Dan. "It provides a needed example of the unity that Christ can bring to people who experience strife and tension. The teachers and staff at Hillcrest are leading a generation of students who will create a future in Jos that is more hopeful than its recent past."

A NEW MODEL FOR SCHOOLING IN ASIA

Asian schools are famous for their academic rigor, and the schools in South Korea are no exception. Because education plays such an important role in future careers and future earning power, South

2

Korea is famous for *hakwons* (also called cram schools), which are private evening schools that help students supplement the education they receive at their daytime schools.

The pressure is so intense that parents pay thousands of dollars a year to enroll high school students in these private schools. What that means for these students is that all day they attend school and then at night go to hakwons, where some of them stay from 5:30 PM to midnight or later as they sit at desks and try to study (and stay awake) the whole time!

A Christian pastor named Dr. Joseph Kim decided that the hakwon system was destroying a generation of young people, so he decided to do something about it. At Central Christian Academy in Suwon, South Korea, students attend a full day of classes, but they are prohibited from attending evening classes.

It was a radical, countercultural idea. How has it turned out?

It has been an amazing success, according to Dan Egeler, who has visited the school. "Instead of the competitive rat race that many Korean students endure," he says, "the students at Central Christian Academy balance study and life. The school graduates are reporting high ranks in high school tests once they matriculate into local high schools [the school goes up to ninth grade]."

Kim is a common name in Korea, but Joseph Kim is the son of a world-famous Christian leader. Following the Korean War, an American GI adopted a young Korean boy named Billy Kim, who came to America to study, earned a doctorate, and accepted Christ. Dr. Billy Kim served as the translator for Billy Graham's Korea crusades and as the senior pastor of Central Baptist Church of Seoul, one of the largest churches in all of Korea. He also served as the president of Baptist World Alliance.

Joseph Kim, like his father, became a pastor. Joseph was content and plenty busy, tending to his church work, but he heard God calling his congregation to start a countercultural Christian school. The church members tithed their income to hire a staff of excellent teachers, not knowing that the school would confront the hakwon approach.

"For Joseph Kim, it was all about the concept of Sabbath," says Dan. "There is a time to study, and students at the school study hard. But there must also be a time for young people to rest or play. Central Christian Academy proves that this kind of God-ordained life balance actually creates a better school experience and better students."

CONFRONTING APARTHEID AND CORRUPTION

I have a photo that Dan Egeler took. It shows two boys—one white and one black—standing together with their arms around each other, their faces bursting out in giant smiles. Dan took the photo of the boys shortly after he found them wrestling in the playground area of The King's School West Rand in a suburb of Johannesburg, South Africa. These first-grade boys are best friends. Their wrestling match was a way for them to burn up energy between classes at the school, a school that has helped break down racial barriers that were institutionalized in South Africa during nearly half a century of racially motivated apartheid rule.

The King's School, the first ACSI-accredited school in South Africa, is looking to the future, not the past, as it seeks to transform the youth of a nation by fostering a climate that promotes unity within the Body of Christ.

Meanwhile, the Dansol High School in Lagos, Nigeria, is a school with a mission: battling the corruption that has been a part of Nigerian life for many years. Here's how the school states its mission on its website: "We are a Christian School dedicated to the training of students who will excel through the wisdom attained from fearing God. Through the blending of biblical principles and modern scholarship, we train students to STAND OUT AND BE DIFFERENT in their generation."

The name *Dansol* comes from the names of two biblical figures—Daniel and Solomon—and the school's curriculum trains students to have the courage of the prophet Daniel and the wisdom of King Solomon. The school focuses on a value system of honesty and integrity that is in sharp contrast to the corruption that has been part of daily life in Nigeria since its independence.

One of the school's teachers says, "We want our students to have the courage of Daniel, the wisdom of Solomon, and a dynamic Christian worldview so they can be 'salt and light'[2] and change our nation."

During a recent visit to the school, Dan Egeler spoke at an assembly of the school's eight hundred students. "I rhetorically asked them, 'How many of you want to be a modern-day Daniel?' " said Dan. "I didn't really expect an answer, but half of the students raised their hands, and a third of them stood up to signify their commitment. I was amazed. I was also impressed by the school's administrators and teachers who regularly pray for every one of the school's students by name. What a powerful image of Christian schooling in action!"

U.S. SCHOOLS

Christian parents in the United States have been deeply involved in educating the young since colonial times, so it's no surprise that today there are thousands of Christian schools in this country. These schools are as varied and diverse as the nation itself.

There are large Christian school systems, like the Christian Academy School System of Louisville, Kentucky, which serves nearly three thousand students in preschool through twelfth grade. The Christian Academy of Louisville High School qualified as a U.S. Department of Education 2010 National Blue Ribbon School.

There are also small schools (enrollments around one hundred or fewer students) that provide quality education. Victory World Christian School is one of these. High tech and high touch—that's the approach that Victory World Christian takes to achieve its goal of equipping students to be strong Christians who are academically prepared to change their world. This small elementary school in Norcross, Georgia, enrolls students from over thirty nations and promotes curiosity, creativity, and character, using cutting-edge technology. Every class has interactive whiteboards, and each child uses a NEO 2 laptop to write, do math drills, take accelerated reading and math quizzes, and "beam" his or her work to the teacher for grading or to classmates for collaborative projects. Students and teachers love this instant feedback. (They love saving all those trees too, because of the school's commitment to conservation activities, which help develop students into good stewards of God's creation.)

And there are stand-alone early education centers, such as Happy Hands Education Center, that make a major difference in young ones' lives. Happy Hands is unique in that it provides specialized Christian schooling for children who have hearing loss and communicative disorders. Its website says, "Our purpose is to empower these special children with confidence, education, life skills and the abilities necessary to achieve all of their dreams…. We provide our students and their families with … a Christian environment, introducing the child to God's love." This educational center is serving many families that have nowhere else to go.

Happy Hands, the only center of its kind in Oklahoma, is not only a pioneer for its own community but also a model for others across the United States to follow. The center serves children aged six weeks to six years, providing a full-time, year-round early intervention program and committing to never turn away a family because of a lack of financial resources (more than 80 percent of the program's families have low incomes). Founded by Al Proo in 1994 in an empty classroom, it moved into a new twenty-thousand-square-foot building in 2010, thanks to a generous grant from the Donald W. Reynolds Foundation. Speaking of the state-of-the-art new facility, Executive Director Proo said, "It's like Moses going through the Red Sea.... When I walk through here, I just see life and kids being successful and parents and their kids being ministered to.... That's what it's all about" (Averill 2010).

Other kinds of Christian schools are those that are known for their powerful athletic programs or their great fine arts programs, schools that have well-established debate teams, schools that have strong computer science departments, and schools that have far-reaching missions programs.

There are schools that are affiliated with churches as well as those that exist independently of churches (though these schools and their students support and are supported by many local churches).

The heart of any school, however, is its people. In the following pages, you will be meeting some of the highly qualified and deeply committed teachers and staff who devote their lives to teaching kids. If there's one trend I've seen in the last two decades, it's the effort by Christian schools to recruit, hire, and train the best educators possible.

Once upon a time, parents who compared Christian schools to nearby government-supported schools might have found that some privately funded Christian schools were weaker than some taxpayer-supported schools. But today, thanks in part to ACSI's demanding requirements for teacher certification and a nationally and internationally recognized school accreditation program, Christian schools are now known for the quality and commitment of their faculty members.

ADDRESSING YOUR CONCERNS

Of course, the people you parents are most concerned about are your own children. As I have visited schools around the world, I have been pleased to see the excitement and happiness on the faces of boys and girls who attend ACSI member schools. If you have ever visited one of our schools yourself, then you know what I'm talking about.

I would love to show you other Christian schools that are changing our world. And I will. In fact, our journey has just begun. I invite you to join me as I continue our tour of Christian schools by examining the key distinctives and advantages these institutions offer to you and your children. As we "travel," I hope that our tour will address whatever concerns you may have about Christian schooling.

Notes

1. An allusion to Matthew 5:14.
2. Another allusion to Matthew 5, this time to verse 13 as well as 14.

HELPING STUDENTS ACHIEVE THEIR FULL POTENTIAL

Our family has always loved our vacations. And I can remember one particular vacation moment that touched me deeply and captured what it means to be a parent.

Bonnie and I were camping with our four children at the Silver Lake Sand Dunes in western Michigan. As we often did, we set off together on a mile-long walk across the dunes from Silver Lake to Lake Michigan. Our youngest daughter, Aubrey, was about five years old at the time, and for part of the walk, I carried her on my shoulders.

But Aubrey was walking on her own as we climbed up the slope of one particularly steep dune. I looked back over my shoulder to make sure she had not fallen behind when I was amazed by what I saw. Aubrey was jumping from one of my footprints to the next. I immediately had one of those parental meltdown moments as I realized my daughter was literally following in my footsteps!

I quickly whispered a prayer to God. "God," I prayed, "it is truly amazing to see my daughter following in my footsteps. *Please*, God, help that be a good thing. Help me so that my footsteps lead her to You."

That pretty much sums up every parent's prayer, doesn't it? We want the best for our children. We want them to enjoy whatever God has planned for them. We want to guide and care for them. And as parents, we want to make sure we are guiding them in the right direction. Deep down we understand our responsibility as stewards of the children God has entrusted to our care. For Bonnie and me, that prayer for our children turned into a conviction that one of the best things we could do was to enroll each of them in Christian schools. Ours is what I call a "cradle to grave" commitment to Christian education. Let me explain what I mean.

A DREAM THAT BECOMES A RESPONSIBILITY

First-time parents have bought millions of copies of the *What to Expect When You're Expecting* (Heidi Murkoff [New York: Workman, 2008]) books. But no matter how much dreaming and preparing the mom and the dad do, it soon becomes obvious that raising children is one of life's supreme responsibilities and greatest challenges.

God entrusts children to parents, at least for a while. During these years, as God's stewards, parents are supposed to care for their children in the best way they know how.

Jesus spoke often about stewardship, and His parables are full of stories that illustrate the difference between "good and faithful" stewards and the other kind (Matthew 25). When it came to raising our children, Bonnie and I committed ourselves to being "good and faithful" (vv. 21 and 23) stewards.

Throughout the Bible, we can see the importance God places on the sacred calling of parents, as stewards of God's most precious possessions, His children.

For instance, John the beloved apostle of Jesus tells us, "I have no greater joy than to hear that my children walk in truth" (3 John 4, KJV). As parents, we feel the same way. From the moment Bonnie and I were married, we agreed that our primary goal for our children and future grandchildren is that each one of them would choose to become a thoroughly prepared and devoted follower of Jesus Christ.

We did everything we could to support this goal and desire. But we also realized we needed help beyond ourselves. Early on we decided that a Christian school education, kindergarten through college, would provide the best means for our children to realize the highest dreams we had for them.

For millennia, godly parents have been doing everything they could to pass on their faith to their children. Moses taught that parents have a sacred duty to the spiritual upbringing of their children:

> Hear, O Israel: The Lord our God, the Lord is one. Love the Lord your God with all your heart and with all your soul and with all your strength. These commandments that I give you today are to be upon your hearts. Impress them on your children. Talk about them when you sit at home and when you walk along the road, when you lie down and when you get up. (Deuteronomy 6:4–7)

What Moses is telling mothers and fathers is that they are responsible to make sure that all the instruction their children receive is consistent with God's truth. Bonnie and I knew that our children would spend many, many more hours learning from their schoolteachers than they would talking with us. Therefore we knew that as stewards of their lives, we needed to focus not only on *who* would teach our children but also *what* our children would be taught and, consequently, *where* they would attend school.

I inherited much of this thinking from my father, who repeatedly passed along to me the words of Joshua when I was still a young boy: "This book of the law shall not depart out of thy mouth; but thou shalt meditate therein day and night, that thou mayest observe to do according to all that is written therein: for then thou shalt make thy way prosperous, and then thou shalt have good success" (1:8, KJV).

Don't all mothers and fathers want success and prosperity for their children? The big question is this: How do you define these things? For us, we knew that no matter how wealthy our children were in material terms, there would not be true success and prosperity for them—either in this life or the next—apart from fulfilling God's purposes for their lives.

Like all parents, we had big dreams for our kids. We wanted the very best for them. We knew that the best meant lives of devotion and service to Jesus Christ. And we knew that the best way to achieve these dreams was to enroll them in Christian schools. We haven't regretted that commitment for a moment.

THE HOME, CHURCH, AND SCHOOL IN CHILD DISCIPLESHIP

In short, what most Christian parents want for their children is for them to be committed, fully prepared disciples of Jesus Christ.

What does it mean to be a disciple of Christ? In its simplest form, it means being a follower of Jesus—to grow to be like Him and to do as He did. That's what it meant when Jesus walked the earth, approached men and women, and gave this invitation: "Come, follow me" (Matthew 19:21).

I believe there are three primary institutions God uses to reach and disciple children: the home, the church, and the school. Each one of these institutions plays an essential role, and when all three work together, they support each other and help children grow up the same way Jesus did: "in wisdom and stature, and in favor with God and men" (Luke 2:52).

Like many Christian educators, I describe these primary institutions as a three-legged stool. When I sit on a stool, I am thankful that its three legs work together to hold me up. I am also grateful when I see a child who is being upheld by the three primary institutions of home, church, and school. These institutions provide the foundation that children need for the rest of their lives.

Fig. 1. The influential three-legged stool.

Ideally, the combined influence of home, church, and school will work together to influence children for Christ. Hopefully, all three will teach the same biblical principles and values so that young people will develop a uniquely Christian worldview.

I believe that Paul's words in his letter to the Ephesians can be applied to this concept of a threefold influence:

> Children, obey your parents in the Lord, for this is right. "Honor your father and mother"—which is the first commandment with a promise—"that it may go well with you and that you may enjoy long life on the earth." Fathers, do not exasperate your children; instead, bring them up in the training and instruction of the Lord....

> Finally, be strong in the Lord and in his mighty power. Put on the full armor of God so that you can take your stand against the devil's schemes. For our struggle is not against flesh and blood, but against the rulers, against the authorities, against the powers of this dark world and against the spiritual forces of evil in the heavenly realms. Therefore

put on the full armor of God, so that when the day of evil comes, you may be able to stand your ground, and after you have done everything, to stand. Stand firm then, with the belt of truth buckled around your waist, with the breastplate of righteousness in place, and with your feet fitted with the readiness that comes from the gospel of peace. In addition to all this, take up the shield of faith, with which you can extinguish all the flaming arrows of the evil one. Take the helmet of salvation and the sword of the Spirit, which is the word of God. (6:1–4, 10–17)

Paul describes the Christian life as a battle against powerful evil forces, and I believe that this very real battle is why children need the three institutions of the home, the church, and the school to work together to support those children's growth and development. We are engaged today in a great spiritual battle for the hearts and minds of our children. Unfortunately, many young people enter it without the necessary preparation and protection.

Parents can't expect young people to succeed as adults in our complex world if their children have received only a Sunday school–level preparation for the challenges and spiritual battles that will confront them. Young people need to see godly values embraced and lived out in their families. They need to be active members in their churches, part of the Body of Christ, in order both to grow their faith and to serve others. And they also need the kind of daily training they could receive at a Christian school—training that would help them apply the values of their faith to everything in life. In Christian schools, Christian teachers integrate faith and learning so that graduates will integrate faith and life.

I believe that one of the reasons so many young people sever their ties to the church once they graduate from high school and enter "adulthood," whether that entrance be at college or in a career, is the disconnect between the secular worldview that students learn in secular schools and the religious training that they receive at home and at church. We—their parents—have neglected to properly prepare them for the challenges and conflicts they will face once they are on their own. As a result, many are mowed down on the battlefield before they even realize that a war is on.

The best solution to these challenges is to provide our sons and daughters with a solid and stable foundation for life. And that foundation is strongest when the three institutions of home, church, and Christian school function together to instill in our children a solid biblical worldview and a strong faith in Jesus Christ.

Parents benefit from pastors and teachers at church and school, people who help moms and dads disciple their children. Churches (including youth groups and other youth ministries) benefit from parents and schoolteachers, both of whom help young people understand and apply biblical principles throughout the week. And schools benefit from families and churches, God-ordained institutions that help introduce children to Christ in their earliest years and who model Christlike living.

So, is any one leg of the stool more important than the other two? No. All three work together in the service of God, as Paul explains in 1 Corinthians:

> There are different kinds of gifts, but the same Spirit. There are different kinds of service, but the same Lord. There are different kinds of working, but the same God works all of them in all men....
>
> The body is a unit, though it is made up of many parts; and though all its parts are many, they form one body. (12:4–6, 12)

The Christian school is not the church, and therefore it should not seek to replace the ministry of the church in the lives of children and families.

But things seem to work best when these three essential institutions overlap appropriately in what they do. For example, a school might interact with families and youth ministries when it is planning a missions trip.

At the same time, some activities are best accomplished solely in one sphere. For example, most families ask the school to teach geography and calculus to their children rather than providing this instruction themselves or expecting the church to do this.

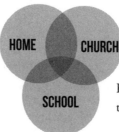

Fig. 2. The overlapping of three essential institutions.

The key point here is that special care must be taken to allow all three institutions to make an impact on children for Christ. All three must work together instead of competing for time and vying for attention as some Christian-school and youth ministries seem to do. Our attitude should be one of cooperation—since we should be like-minded in what we want for young people—rather than one of competition for resources.

Christian educator Glen Schultz writes in his book, *Kingdom Education: God's Plan for Educating Future Generations*, that Christian education is the process by which we should be "leading a child to Christ" and "building a child up in Christ" so that the child will be equipped to serve Christ (1998, 29).

I believe that this process works best when parents, church, and school work together to make disciples of our children.

GOD'S WORK AND OUR WORK

I have heard some critics of Christian schools claim that discipleship is the work of the home or the church and that academics is the work of schools. The way Bonnie and I see it, we need the support of the church and the Christian school to help us achieve our mission as parents: that our children will grow in and demonstrate love for God, one another, and others.

One of my favorite authors is Jerry Bridges. He explores this issue of responsibility in his book *Trusting God Even When Life Hurts*. Here's what he says: "We must depend upon God to do *for* us what we cannot do for ourselves. We must, to the same degree, depend on Him to *enable us* to do what we must do for ourselves" (1988, 112). He also says that "God usually works through means, and He intends that we use the means He has placed at our disposal" (110).

Bridges writes that some Christians are tempted to believe that "God's sovereignty negates any responsibility of ours to live responsible and prudent lives" (1988, 105). I believe that God is sovereign, but I also believe that He has called parents to be good and faithful stewards of their children's lives. Parents who turn to good Bible-believing churches and solid Christian schools to help them raise their children aren't turning their back on their responsibilities. They are trying to fulfill those responsibilities as best they can!

I recently had a heartbreaking conversation with a dear friend for whom the duties of being a father have been very challenging. My friend has two children from a previous marriage. He has since remarried, and he and his wife now have their own beautiful infant daughter.

He explained in some detail the grief he has experienced because his older children have not chosen to love and serve God. He has also confessed to me some of his failings as a father that he fears may have resulted in prodigal children. He expressed his deep desire that his young daughter not go down the same path that his older children took.

As we talked, he also told me that he is not currently attending church regularly or spending time in the Word of God. Between the pressures of his new family and of his career, these things have slipped from their important positions. I didn't need to tell him that I felt he was neglecting one of his primary duties as a father. He had acknowledged as much himself.

Parents want what's best for their children, but we're not perfect. We don't always know what to do or say. And sometimes we fail to model Christlike living for our kids.

That's one reason I am so thankful for Christian schools: parents *aren't* perfect. The loving and caring men and women who serve at Christian schools can help provide solid biblical teaching and examples in our children's lives. This way, the schooling leg of the stool provides extra support for the home, or family, leg when it wobbles a bit and proves not as strong as it could or should be.

LIVING THE DREAM

Being a parent is one of the most challenging roles a person can take on. And today parents have many options when it comes to educating their children. I believe the choice of where to send children to school is one of the biggest decisions parents must make.

As a father, I have never regretted my decision to enroll my four children in Christian schools. All four of them grew in practical knowledge, in spiritual wisdom, and in a deep love for God during their years at Christian schools. And now, that positive input continues to inform and influence their lives.

No two families are the same. So what about yours?

Do you want your children to experience the very best of what God has for them? Do you hope to be a good and faithful steward of the children God has entrusted to your care? If so, I pray that you will choose Christian schooling for them.

DR. DEREK KEENAN ON THE VALUE OF CHRISTIAN EDUCATION

As a father, church elder, lifelong educator, and former administrator of a Christian school, I can see the importance Christian schooling has had in the lives of many young people.

When I dig deeper and explore what it is that has made many of these young people so successful and so confident in their faith, I can see that it all began with parents who made a conscious choice to front-load their children's faith development when their children were at an early age.

As Nicholas Wolterstorff, the respected Christian philosopher from Yale University, put it, education is about preparing young people for life (2002). And Christian education prepares young people for a particular kind of life that we call Christian.

I inherited my love for God and my love for learning from my father. I grew up in Ireland, where my father was a pastor. Our family had very little means, but we lived daily in the joy of the Lord.

Every evening we would enjoy lively and deep conversation around the dinner table about what we were reading. We explored current ideas to see how they related (or didn't relate) to the Bible. When it came time for me to attend college, I had strong encouragement from both my parents, who had equipped me with the ability and desire to contextualize ideas and measure them by God's Word.

Today not all children enjoy this kind of environment. That's why I tell parents that the decision about where they send their children to school is really a fifteen-thousand-hour question. That's about how many hours young people are going to spend with their various teachers between kindergarten and graduation from high school.

I have seen many cases in which teachers at Christian schools seek out teachable moments with young people that affect those young people for a lifetime. For example, one fourth grader mentioned in class that his grandmother had recently died. His Christian teacher explored this issue in a way that was sensitive and biblically informed. I am not sure a teacher in a secular school would have been able to use this teachable moment in so powerful a way.

There come times in the life of every young person when he or she asks questions about the meaning and purpose of life. This is an opportunity that is of limited duration. I always wanted my children to be around caring Christian teachers when these questions were being discussed. The impact of Christian education varies for each student, but parents who desire to see their children follow God should consider the positive and long-term impact it could have in the lives of their own children.

Derek Keenan is the vice president for Academic Affairs for ACSI. He is an author who has a doctorate in educational leadership from Nova University and a master's in education from the University of South Florida. He has done postdoctoral studies at Florida State University.

WHAT'S "CHRISTIAN" ABOUT CHRISTIAN SCHOOLS?

The earliest followers of Jesus were first referred to as "Christians" in the cosmopolitan Greek city of Antioch (Acts 11:26). Antioch was the capital of the Roman province of Syria and an important center of commerce that was home to Greeks, Romans, Jews, and many other groups, so it only made sense that believers needed a name by which they could be called.

Today believers in Christ (statistics range from under 1 billion to almost 2 billion believers) are still referred to as Christians. People also apply the word *Christian* to things, including Christian books, Christian rock bands, and even Christian diet programs.

Can *things* truly be Christian? Not according to some theologians. These thinkers say that the only entities that deserve to be called Christian are *people* who have accepted Jesus as Savior and determined to live their lives according to His teaching and example.

Even so, I believe there's a solid case to be made for using the term *Christian school* to describe the thousands of ACSI member schools around the world. That's because the people who work at these schools and teach the millions of children who attend share a commitment to Jesus and to instilling His truth in students' minds and hearts.

In this chapter, I am going to answer the question, What makes a Christian school Christian? As you will see, it's not the bricks that make up the building or the asphalt in the parking lot or even the cross on the sign out front that determines whether a school is Christian. It's something much deeper and more powerful than that.

If you seriously examine Christian schools, as I have over the years, and peel back their layers as you would the layers of an onion, what you will see at the core of everything these schools do is Jesus, who was not only the greatest teacher the world has ever known but also the world's only Savior and Redeemer.

All secular educational institutions are based on a human being or the ideas of a human being, whether that be a particular thinker, a specific school of thought, or a unique approach to education. But the foundation of Christian schools is Jesus' life and message and the teaching of the Bible.

But the reality of this biblical foundation doesn't mean that the only thing our students study is the Bible. Far from it. Christian school students delve deeply into literature, math, science, history, music, geography, grammar, psychology, art, and sociology, but during the learning process, their teachers help them continually connect the dots between the various academic disciplines and the eternal nature of God's truth.

One term many Christian educators use to describe what we do, the kind of education we offer, is *holistic*. Some people may think this term is new, but it has a long history. As *The American Heritage Dictionary* tells us, the word refers to approaches "emphasizing the importance of the whole and the interdependence of its parts."[1] What this definition means in the typical Christian school is that no matter what the subject is, it will be taught within the larger context of biblical principles and God's will for our lives.

Does a person need to attend a Christian school to be a Christian? Of course not. The believers in Antioch were known as followers of Jesus before they received any formal Christian schooling. But today we live in a complex world, where various worldviews are vying for young people's hearts and minds. Parents who want to give their children plenty of opportunities to integrate faith with classroom lessons will be able to see the distinctively Christian nature of what we do.

Our goal is to work with the committed educators who serve in Christian schools worldwide in order to help students become "thinking disciples"—disciples who connect the conviction that Jesus is Lord to the principles of science or algebra or public speaking that will serve them throughout their lives.

ONE PURPOSE, MANY PATTERNS

There's no single way to do Christian schooling, as I have seen myself by visiting many of our member schools throughout the world.

For example, some schools require that all enrolled students personally profess faith in Jesus Christ. Others practice "open enrollment," allowing students to attend regardless of faith profession.

Some schools require that at least one parent of every student claim to be a committed Christian. Other schools focus mainly on the students' beliefs instead of the parents'.

Of the Christian schools I have seen, virtually all of them enforce stringent codes of conduct for employees and students alike. Typically these codes of conduct are based on biblical principles and on the belief that employment or attendance at these schools is a unique privilege that carries with it certain moral responsibilities. (But there's no uniform conduct code used by all ACSI member schools.)

The best way to find out the DNA of your own local Christian school is to do some homework. You can start with a school website—which expresses a school's core convictions and guiding principles—to learn more about the Christian schools near you, or you can visit the ACSI website at www.acsi.org for a listing of ACSI member schools, whose websites you can explore.

I also encourage you to contact the administrators and teachers at your local Christian school and ask them to tell you about the values and principles that guide their daily work with students.

If you do this research, here's what I think you will find: The men and women who run and staff Christian schools come from a variety of backgrounds and Christian traditions. They have a wide range of opinions about how best to teach students and what techniques work the best.

But there's one thing they all agree on. Jesus Christ is at the center of everything they do. And it's a desire to see students know Jesus better, love Him more deeply, and grow to effectively serve Him wholeheartedly that inspires and motivates them.

THE WORLDVIEW DISTINCTIVE

There was a time in the history of the United States when the goals and purposes of education and the basic principles of the Judeo-Christian tradition were nearly identical. Textbooks clearly reflected biblical truth. Prayer was a regular and widely accepted practice in schools. But those days are gone in the United States. Local, state, and national policies on education now reflect the secular perspective that is so pervasive. Once, Christian parents could largely feel secure when sending their children to public schools, confident that their faith and values would be respected. Today secular private and public schools, including charter schools, are based on naturalistic biological evolution and secular humanistic philosophy, both of which deny the existence of a God and call into question the very foundations of Judeo-Christian tradition.

But outside the United States, policy on education varies widely from country to country. For example, students in the countries of Germany, Italy, Australia, and the Democratic Republic of the Congo, to name just a few, continue to receive religious instruction in their public schools, which are funded by the government. Still, there's one thing that makes Christian schooling supremely important, no matter where the schools are located. This one thing can be summarized in one word: *worldview.*

Christian leader Chuck Colson addressed this topic in a 2009 edition of his popular BreakPoint Commentary: "Yes, the evangelical movement is growing, which is good, but numbers don't mean everything. For example, a new Barna survey shows that only 19 percent of evangelicals hold a consistently biblical worldview."

Why should this surprise us? The majority of Christian young people today are educated in secular schools that teach a secular worldview. And many of their parents fail to embrace a deep and balanced understanding of Christian teaching. Colson goes on to write the following:

> What this tells me is that we're growing in numbers, but we've got to do a better job making disciples....
>
> I can't help but think of William Wilberforce, the English parliamentarian who led a small band of believers to eradicate the British slave trade. These men and women, inspired by God, shared their resources, talents, and faith, and not only put an end to a great evil, but they also formed the heart of a movement that quite literally sparked revival and transformed the culture of Britain. It began with a handful of the faithful.

Just think what God might do with 34 percent of the American population calling themselves evangelicals—if those evangelicals recapture their first love, present a winsome witness, and do the good works God has prepared for us to do. (2009)

Christian education is about much more than memorizing Bible verses. It's about applying biblical truths to all the philosophies and issues and challenges of our time so that our students will have hearts aflame with love for God and minds empowered by the truth of God.

No matter where you live or what your local public school policy on religious instruction in school, this emphasis on connecting the dots between the education of children and their faith has been one of the central tenets of Christian education for twenty centuries.

So what is it that makes Christian schools distinctive? It is the worldview—squarely centered on the person of Jesus Christ, who is the Truth (John 14:6), and on the foundation provided by the written Word of God—which is absolute truth (2 Timothy 2:15). We are not merely excellent private schools; we are private Christian schools that exist for a very specific purpose. And ACSI exists as an association of those distinct Christian schools to bring glory to God as Christian school educators around the world make thoroughly prepared disciples of Jesus Christ. And how do those educators make such disciples? By building all they do upon the firm foundation of the Word of God and by focusing on God's Son, Jesus Christ. In short, our desire is that Christian school students will embrace a thoroughly biblical, Christian worldview and will then live it out.

THE BOOK ABOVE ALL BOOKS

When I turned sixteen years old, my father gave me a new Bible. Inside the cover, he wrote these words: "Son, this book will keep you from sin, and sin will keep you from this book." He also inscribed these words of Joshua, who led the Israelite people after the death of Moses: "This book of the law shall not depart out of thy mouth; but thou shalt meditate therein day and night, that thou mayest observe to do according to all that is written therein: for then thou shalt make thy way prosperous, and then thou shalt have good success" (1:8, KJV).

As a child, I knew that the Bible was a special book, a book above all other books. Unfortunately, some Christians seem to believe that the Bible is merely a "religious" book full of arcane and abstract teachings on obscure religious behavior. But I am convinced that the Bible enlightens all of life. The question is, How are we going to apply this book to our lives?

The Bible itself tells us that its words are inspired by God (2 Timothy 3:16, KJV). No other "holy book" contains God's message to humankind. No other book presents justification by grace through faith in Jesus, who, as John tells us, is "the way, the truth, and the life" (John 14:6).

In *Living by the Book*, Howard and William Hendricks argue that the Bible is not written to satisfy our curiosity. It is written to help us conform to Christ's image. "Dusty Bibles always lead to dirty lives," they write (1991, 10).

The Bible is not one book. It is a library written by more than forty authors from all different walks of life over a period of about sixteen hundred years. The golden thread that runs through all of Scripture is God's plan of redemption.

Psalm 119:105 (NKJV) says, "Your word is a lamp to my feet and a light to my path." Verse 128 says, "All Your precepts ... I consider to be right; I hate every false way." And Psalm 32:8 says, "I will instruct you and teach you in the way you should go; I will guide you with My eye."

Simply put, the Bible is more than a collection of words and stories. It is a guidebook to life that is written by the Creator of life. And by helping students read, understand, and use this book, Christian schools are guiding students on a path of meaning and service in both this life and the next.

THE INTEGRATION OF FAITH AND LEARNING

Christian schools focus on effective teaching and student learning so that students will be prosperous and successful in life as evaluated by God's measure of success and prosperity. (For more on this point, see the next chapter.) So there's more to Christian schooling than strong academics.

One of the distinctives of Christian education is that students understand that the truth of every subject, the written curriculum, emanates from the absolute truth of God's Word.

It's important for students to know how to complete algebra problems, conduct science experiments, and write research papers. But it's even more important that they learn to address the deeper life questions that are a continual part of both life and education.

Whether students are immersed in literature or history, or whether they are more focused on issues and challenges in life outside the classroom, young people regularly ask questions such as the following:
- Where did I come from?
- Why am I here?
- What is the purpose of life?
- Is there a God?
- When does life begin?
- Is there life after death?

- What is true justice?
- What responsibility do I have for the welfare of others?
- What is a family?
- What are the ethical limits of technological advances?

Questions like these arise whether young people attend a Christian school or a public school. The difference is found in the kinds of answers students will receive when they discuss these questions in the classroom or in the hallway.

That's perhaps the biggest distinctive of Christian schooling. It's not just about the academic subjects; it's about the perspective from which students are encouraged to view the life lessons that they receive along the way.

If you want your children to grow up learning how to naturally connect the dots between God's truth and every other topic or subject that they will encounter throughout their lives, I encourage you to consider enrolling them in a Christian school.

Although Christian schools certainly aren't perfect, they are focused on the Someone who is. And that Person can make all the difference in the world!

Note

1. *The American Heritage Dictionary*, fourth edition (Boston, MA: Houghton Mifflin Company, 2000; updated 2009) definition for *holistic* can be found at http://www.thefreedictionary.com/holistic.

A LIFETIME OF LESSONS
BY DANNY OERTLI

I can still remember the morning my mom drove me to Colorado Springs Christian School [CSCS] and dropped me off for my first day of classes at my new school. My dad had just begun work as the pastor of a local church, and my parents had decided it was best for me to attend a Christian school.

With wide eyes and knocking knees, I walked into Mrs. Rothberg's sixth-grade classroom, where the first surprise was that week's Bible memory verse.

I was expecting to work on math, English, social studies—just like my last school. But memorizing Scripture? Initially I was so slow at memorization that you could have timed my progress with an Egyptian sundial. But before long the weekly verses made their way from the chalkboard into my head and, eventually, into my heart.

Thank you, Mrs. Rothberg, for faithfully watering our minds and souls with God's Word.

The transition from elementary school to junior high was like merging onto a freeway with a horse and buggy. Thankfully I had Mr. Hestermann to guide me along the way. Mr. H. was both the principal and the junior high basketball coach. In addition to teaching us how to play ball and become more disciplined, Mr. H. helped us become young men.

Thank you, Mr. H., for caring about me beyond basketball and for faithfully shaping my character. To this day, I can still hear your voice encouraging me to do my best, both on the court and off.

Mr. Wallace was a gentle giant of a high school teacher who helped me fall in love with history. In the pages of the past, Mr. Wallace found fascinating stories about great men and women of faith who honored the name of God. Each class period felt like an adventure as we journeyed together to exotic lands and periods.

Mr. Wallace also taught me deeper lessons that would later have a profound impact on me, though I didn't realize it at the time. Tragically, his son died while I was in high school. Mr. Wallace was absent for a few days to grieve with his family. When he returned to the classroom, two things were clear: (1) he was still in pain, but (2) God was still good.

Thank you, Mr. Wallace, for teaching us powerful lessons about hope in the midst of sorrow.

Soon I would experience my own sorrow. My cousin was brutally murdered during my senior year of high school. This family tragedy took its toll on me, and I missed a week of school and track practice.

When I showed up at that weekend's track meet, I was tired and unfocused. Our coach, Mr. Rodine, approached me and put an arm around my shoulder. "Hey," he said, "no one expects anything of you today. If you only make it halfway around the track, I'll meet you there and we can go grab a hot dog."

Thank you, Mr. Rodine, for being a coach *and* a friend.

Unfortunately, I was to experience heart-wrenching tragedy again in my life. When I was 30, my wife, Cyndi, passed away after a long battle with cancer. I was left with two small children and an uncertain future.

Late one evening I received a phone call. It had been years since I had heard this voice, but I immediately recognized it. It was Mr. Sciacca, a Bible teacher who was as popular for his classes as he was for his extracurricular counseling sessions with students in the hallways after class was over. That night on the phone, Mr. Sciacca did what he had always done in his class; he gently guided me to Jesus—the Teacher, the Savior, and the Healer.

Thank you, Mr. Sciacca, for your continual and consistent impact in my life.

It's been more than twenty years since I graduated from CSCS, but I continue to witness the life-changing impact of Christian schooling. Since graduating from college I have worked as a musician, making records and traveling around the country to perform. And I frequently have the opportunity to play at chapels for Christian schools.

Often, while waiting to be introduced, I sneak a look at the students, who seem so young, so full of life, so full of questions. I also look at the staff. Do these hardworking men and women realize the influence they have on students like me? Do they realize how much we—and God—appreciate what they do?

I'm remarried now, and this morning my wife, Rayna, and I dropped off our three kids at Southeast Christian School in Denver. As I watched my daughter Grace greet her teacher in the parking lot, I said this little prayer: "Thank you, God, for Christian schools."

And thank you, Mr. O'Reilly, for helping my daughter Grace after school with her work. It will not be forgotten.

Danny Oertli is an accomplished singer, songwriter, and author. He currently lives in Parker, Colorado, with his wife, Rayna, and their three children. For booking information and CD and book orders, please visit www.dannyoertli.com.

WORLD-CLASS LEARNING

I can still remember the day when it was decided (and not by me!) that I would be attending a Christian school.

I was sixteen years old, and my mom had pulled me into our living room for a talk about her concerns. I wasn't in any serious trouble at home or at school, but both she and my father were concerned about how I was growing up. I seemed to be wandering through life rather than choosing good goals and pursuing them with discipline.

"Even the pastor is concerned," she told me. That certainly got my attention. But nothing grabbed me as much as her next sentence: "We need to enroll you in a Christian school."

I knew that our church, First Baptist Church of Elkhart, Indiana, ran a Christian school, and I knew some local kids who attended there. They seemed OK to me. But attending Christian school was the furthest thing from my mind. And, frankly, I wanted it to stay that way.

"There is no way I will ever go to a Christian school!" I told her.

Mom remained calm. "Brian, your father and I have talked about this," she said. "We think a Christian school would be best for you.

And even though we would have to scrimp to pay tuition for you to attend, we feel it would be well worth it. We want you to know that you don't have to do this if you don't want to. But your father and I have a simple request. At least go and talk to the pastor about it."

I liked our pastor, so I was glad to talk to him. But as we drove to his office at the church, all kinds of crazy questions went through my head. If I attended a Christian school, would I study the Bible all day long? Would I ever get to see any of my friends who attended other schools? And would I have to be a pastor myself once I graduated?

Our pastor, Daniel Gelatt, was kind and patient, as always. He explained how the leadership of the church saw the school—as a natural extension of their ministry to families and young people. But it was my mother who surprised me.

"Pastor, we believe sending Brian to Elkhart Christian Academy [ECA] is the *right* thing to do, but we're not sure it's the *best* thing for Brian," she said. "After all, Brian is gifted in math and science. Do you think he will get the best education here? And will he be able to take calculus at ECA?"

Pastor Gelatt didn't hesitate. "I promise you that Brian will get the best education here," he said. "And yes," he continued, "Brian will learn calculus."

That is how, in the span of a few hours, my life took a different course. And I can't begin to tell you how thankful I am for that. Decades later, as I write these words, I can't stop thinking about the dedicated ECA teachers, coaches, and administrators who made my time there so enjoyable and beneficial.

I praise the Lord for parents who loved me enough to send me to a Christian school, and for a pastor who cared enough about me to meddle in my personal life!

Now, as I get to see Christian schools all over the world, I wish I could talk to every young man or young woman who has the same kinds of questions about Christian schools that I had when I was younger.

Whether you're a student or a parent, my message to you in this chapter is simple: the education students receive at Christian schools is truly world-class.

The men and women who work for Christian schools care deeply about Christ, but their commitment doesn't end there. They care deeply about their students, and they want to impart the best education possible.

Over the decades of my service as an educator, I have witnessed how Christian schooling prepares students for careers, service, life, and further academic study. And I believe Christian schools do this better than any other institution around.

A SUPERIOR FOUNDATION

Christian schools aren't part of the public, government-run educational systems around the globe that enroll most of the world's schoolchildren. But being separate doesn't mean Christian schools are substandard. In fact, I believe that most Christian schools deliver results that are superior to those of the public schools.

In order for you to see what I mean, I want you to listen to the story of Taylor Smith, the senior vice president of ACSI USA. While I was a child studying at Elkhart Christian Academy, Taylor was growing up and experiencing the effects of a flawed and racist approach to schooling known as "separate but equal." Here's his story:

> I grew up when America was racially segregated, and I attended an all-black school in Stanton, Virginia, from first grade through graduation. In 1956 Rosa Parks had refused to give up her seat on a bus, but in the 1960s I was still riding in the back of the bus in my hometown.

> The good thing was that just about all my teachers were committed believers who prayed in our classrooms. These dedicated teachers inspired me to make education my career. And it was while working on a doctorate at Ohio State University that I had my first classroom teaching experience in a Columbus-area middle school. I immediately fell in love with teaching and have been an educator ever since.

> In 1983 I began working as superintendent of nearby Worthington Christian Schools, where I served for the next twenty-one years. During this time, our entire staff worked to educate students in a consistent way that balanced their social, physical, and spiritual needs.

> Education that was distinctively Christian happened on the athletic field as well as in the classroom, as my son Dwayne [Smith 2009] pointed out in his book, *The Christian Athlete: Honoring God Through Sports*. Coaches have a different kind of relationship with students than teachers do. But I am convinced that coaching is teaching by other means. And in an age when professional athletes can be bad role models, I celebrate the good work Christian coaches do.

> One question I learned to ask during my educational studies was, What are the foundations and assumptions of each educational philosophy? For me, the thing that makes Christian schooling unique is its foundation. You can see what I mean by comparing the two pyramids in figure 3.

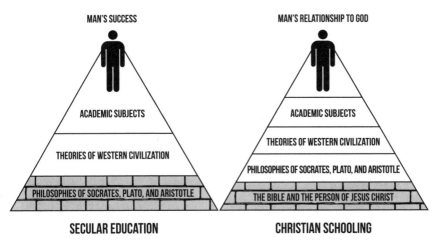

Fig. 3. Two philosophies of education.

Every educational philosophy is based on a set of assumptions about human nature, the mind, education, and the purpose of life.

In most cases secular education is based on one particular theorist or body of work. For example, pyramid 1 illustrates a secular educational model based on the foundation provided by thinkers like Socrates, Plato, and Aristotle. The next higher level of the pyramid traces this influence through other key thinkers and theories of Western civilization. And on top of these foundations, come all the academic disciplines and subjects.

Pyramid 2 shows that Christian education teaches academic subjects as well but that the difference is the foundation. The foundation of Christian schooling is Jesus Christ and the truth and wisdom of Scripture. Students at our schools still study the early philosophers, world civilizations, and all the academic disciplines, but they do so on the basis of a solid foundation that is unique. If the principles of the Bible and the philosophies and writings of man disagree, then the Bible is right and the others are wrong.

Today parents have much more choice in schooling than I had when I was a student. One of the alternatives is charter schools. After attending Christian schools for sixteen years, my son Derek, following graduation from college, now teaches at a charter school. He is a good teacher and he enjoys his work, but because he is teaching in a public school,[1] he lacks the freedom he used to have to share insights from the Bible or a personal faith perspective. On the other hand, my oldest son, Dwayne, taught in a Christian school for fourteen years and had the freedom to share with his students from the Word of God and life-on-life applications of biblical principles.

That's part of what I love so much about Christian schooling. It educates students in the important subjects and does so in a balanced way. Christian teachers also have a powerful opportunity to change lives because they see your children more often than your church's pastor or youth pastor does.

I have seen many changes in my life and have witnessed a variety of educational philosophies come and go. The more I see, the more I believe in the importance of Christian schooling, which provides students with a solid foundation in a balanced and positive way.

ACADEMIC EXCELLENCE IN ACTION

I wish you could see some of the exciting things I see as I travel and visit Christian schools.

One example of an impressive institution is Chinese Christian Schools in San Leandro, California. Although 60 percent of the students at Chinese Christian Schools do not speak English as their primary language when they start their studies at the school, these students have scored in the top 10 percent nationally on the *SAT 10* (*Stanford Achievement Test, Tenth Edition*) since 2000. This was one reason the school was recognized by the U.S. Department of Education in 2003 as a National Blue Ribbon School.

By the time of high school graduation, 80 percent of the school's students will have taken an honors or an AP (advanced placement) class, and over half will have earned the AP Scholar designation (by obtaining a score of three or above on three or more AP exams). Their average composite score on the *SAT Reasoning Test* is 1787 over the past three years, and in the past five years, they have earned over 25 CIF (California Interscholastic Federation) Scholastic Championship Team Awards. They have one of the top three team-grade-point averages in the entire North Coast Section for their sport.

Since the inception of Chinese Christian Schools in 1979, it has graduated 698 students, all of whom have gone on to college or gone into the military. Ninety percent have been accepted into four-year universities, and about 25 percent go on to do graduate work after college.

Another impressive institution is Tree of Life Christian Schools. I recently received the following story about Tree of Life from Kimberly Peeks, an educator, a wife, and a mother of five from Columbus, Ohio:

> I am a product of the public school system, and I determined upon graduation from high school that I would do what I could to make a positive impact in the lives of others by becoming a teacher so I could give back to the same school system that helped shape me to be the person that I am today.

> And as for my own children, I thought that if public school was good enough for me, surely it was good enough for my children. Three generations of women in my family had graduated from the same high school. I wanted my daughters to be that fourth generation.

> Unfortunately, the school that I loved became an academic emergency. Test scores fell. Students failed to meet state standards in

core subjects. The educational dreams of many young students whom I knew personally were shattered because of underperforming institutions.

In 2006 my husband and I made one of the greatest decisions in the lives of our children by enrolling them at Tree of Life Christian Schools. The faculty and staff immediately embraced our entire family, and our children are now receiving a quality education in a safe and loving environment.

I have seen how our children are challenged in every aspect of their educational experience. What my husband and I instill at home is being reinforced at school, and I am most grateful for that. They are thriving mentally, physically, emotionally, and spiritually.

And our family is not the only one to benefit. Thanks to Ohio's statewide EdChoice Scholarship Program, fourteen thousand students trapped in failed public schools were eligible to receive vouchers that provided their parents the opportunity to exercise school choice. In the fall of 2006, Tree of Life Christian Schools welcomed twenty-five of these EdChoice students into our school family. Over the past five years, that number has grown to more than one hundred students, representing about one-sixth of our student population. Most of these children have flourished academically, spiritually, and socially.

BEING CREATIVE FOR THE CREATOR

In this chapter, we have seen how Christian schools pursue excellence in academics. I also want to share some of the good things I have seen in the creative arts.

If you are a parent of a student, you have probably had the opportunity to attend an assembly or a concert during which students sing, play music, or act out dramatic roles. I don't know about you, but when I see these performances, tears come to my eyes because of the joy and excitement at seeing Christian students excel in the creative arts.

The commitment to arts education begins with administrators, teachers, and parents who make it happen in local schools. One good example of such a commitment is evident at an ACSI school in Redmond, Washington—The Bear Creek School, which offers a Shakespeare Immersion Program that begins in kindergarten and continues through high school. This fine arts experience allows students at various grade levels to investigate and theatrically experience how aspects of character, cultural context, power, and social status affect and potentially alter life outcomes. The program provides a window into the world of others, an exceptional platform to teach and expose the condition of the human heart while making substantive connections to biblical themes.

In the kindergarten through third-grade classes, the children learn plotlines of four Shakespearean plays. They discuss character traits and learn about rhyme, meter, and the syntax of language. In fourth grade, the students receive a broad exposure to Elizabethan culture through English history, the history of drama in England, the issues of gender and class structure, the life of William Shakespeare, and the historical significance of each play. By sixth grade, the students have performed in vignettes of several plays, and this participation culminates in a full-cast performance of *Julius Caesar*. And by the end of their high school journey, the students have experienced a substantial repertoire and developed a deep appreciation for the beauty and emotion, the tragedy and comedy, and the conflict and treachery illustrated throughout the dramatic works they've studied and performed. Through an intentionally sequenced immersion in the masterful works of Shakespeare, the students not only read about but also virtually live out the earthly and eternal consequences of the Shakespearean characters' actions and choices.

You can probably imagine how much work on the part of the whole school community goes into an arts education program like the one at Bear Creek. I believe that our Creator is pleased with these efforts that are designed to foster the God-given creativity of our students. In this way and so many others, Christian schools are providing a world-class education to children and young people around the world.

If you or your children have ever felt the same uncertainty about Christian education that I did way back when I was a youngster, I invite you to take a closer look at one of the fine Christian schools near you. Catch a sporting event or enjoy a concert or a play. If you do, you will be amazed by the world-class education personified in the students attending these schools. You'll see that we are pursuing a powerful combination of academic excellence and Christian conviction. And as I look at the world around me, I know that this type of education is one of the best contributions we can make to our future.

Note

1. All charter schools in the United States are public schools. They are supposedly "tuition free," but none are truly free, because all charter schools are funded by taxpayer dollars (as are all other U.S. public schools).

THE HUMAN TOUCH

For more than a quarter century, Dan Stroup has taught middle school Bible classes in Indianapolis at Heritage Christian School, which, like most ACSI member schools, requires all students to take a Bible class every year. What is it that keeps Dan motivated after teaching more than thirty thousand classes?

It's simple. He loves kids and he loves God. And it's his passion for helping his students understand God's Word and apply it to their lives that inspires his teaching.

"I had graduated from a Christian school and later from Bible college," says Dan. "I had some very good teachers who helped me see that the Bible is practical and useful for daily life. And I really wanted to be able to teach that to others. I didn't feel I would have the opportunity to do that in a public school, so I looked for an opportunity to teach in a Christian school."

Dan works hard in the classroom and spends extra time before and after class in preparation and grading student papers. But it's what Dan does *beyond* those standard teaching tasks that's even more amazing. Once a year Dan writes a personalized birthday letter to all his students—past and present.

He started writing birthday letters to his students on October 1, 1985, when he sent his first letter to a student named Connie. Since then, he's written more than thirty-three thousand personalized letters to his twenty-five hundred Bible students, according to a short article in the *AARP Bulletin* (Tucker 2010) and other publications. Each letter includes a Bible verse intended to help guide and comfort the recipient.

"Writing the letters started as a way to have a more personal interaction with my students on an individual basis," he says. "I only have forty-five minutes a day in the classroom, so the individual time is limited. I was looking for a way to touch their lives in a more personal way."

In his letters, Dan communicates with students about messages in the Bible that apply to the issues and challenges in their daily lives. And according to a TV news story about Dan (viewable on YouTube[1]), the students appreciate this personal touch.

"Every year, it makes my birthday extra special," said Aka Egwu in a story for the NBC affiliate in Indianapolis (Swan 2009). Aka took Dan's Bible class in 1997, and he has kept nearly every letter. "It's a tradition," Aka told *Eyewitness News*. "He always gives you a little bit of wisdom.... And he really cares about where you're going and how you're living your life."

Dan stays in touch with former students like Aka. It's all part of a personal commitment to teaching that extends beyond the walls of the classroom.[2]

"Families send their children to Christian schools because they want their children to have a better knowledge of God's Word," says Dan. "They want their children to know God's plan for their lives. I see what I do—both in the classroom and outside the classroom—as a way for me to help the parents to instruct their children, teach them, and correct them in the ways of righteousness. It's a privilege for me to be able to come in and teach these young people that the Bible is God's practical guide for their lives and is something that can be used today and forever. It's a practical thing that can be used for the rest of their lives."

TEACHING IS PERSONAL

When I served for nearly a decade as superintendent at Heritage Christian School, I had the privilege of working alongside Dan Stroup. And as amazing as his story is, it illustrates some of the core values that unite all Christian schoolteachers around the world.

As Christians, we have a unique perspective on the importance of personalized teaching. That's because our faith is based on the example of the master teacher Jesus Christ. Jesus called His disciples to follow Him, and He spent the next three years pouring Himself into these students.

When they first met Jesus, these disciples weren't geniuses. They weren't men of wealth or power or privilege. They weren't necessarily people who would have been recognized by their peers as individuals who were destined to succeed.

But after three years with their teacher, these disciples went on to teach many others. And in the process of doing this, they changed the world.

As parents, we all want our children to grow up understanding and applying the Word of God. And many of us also pray and dream that our children will grow up to make the world a more godly and positive place.

I am convinced that Christian schoolteachers like Dan Stroup hold the key to producing the kinds of godly, loving, and world-changing children who will be needed to serve and lead both in the Church and in the world in the years ahead. That is why teachers like Dan Stroup are the gold in the bank of every Christian school. They are the living curriculum, and the Scriptures teach us that when students are fully taught, they will be like their teachers (Luke 6:40).

BALANCING HEART, MIND, AND CHARACTER

There are more than 2.5 million students attending over twenty-two thousand ACSI member schools in more than one hundred countries around the world. And it's the more than thirty thousand ACSI-certified teachers and administrators who are responsible for teaching the classes and managing the accredited schools.

In many ways, these hardworking men and women are the foundation of everything we do. They represent both Christ and the children's parents in the classrooms and hallways of our schools. They are the essential human link that makes the connection between your children and the values and knowledge that we all desire to pass on.

Anyone could set up a few chairs in a garage or a basement and call it a Christian school. But ACSI member schools must meet a higher standard—and ACSI-accredited schools an even higher standard.[3]

Merry Clark has been the director of Academic Services at ACSI for eleven years. She leads ACSI's Certification Department, which helps us make sure that teachers and administrators in Christian schools combine heart, mind, and character. Previously, Merry served twenty-six years as a teacher, an administrator, and even a school cofounder.

Anyone who wants to teach or serve in an ACSI-accredited Christian school must demonstrate competencies and credentials in the following areas:

- **Academic training**—All teachers and administrators must have a bachelor's degree and the required eighteen to thirty-three semester hours in educational studies and student teaching. (The type and number of hours depends on whether the applicant works as an administrator or a teacher and whether the applicant serves in an elementary or secondary school.) This course work must be from a regionally accredited or ACSI-recognized institution. "We will not accept course work or degrees from 'degree mills' or institutions that lack the proper validation," says Merry.
- **Christian credentials**—Because teaching in a Christian school is a unique calling that carries with it unique demands, we also require that all teachers and administrators have training in biblical studies and in the Christian philosophy of education.
- **Character**—Every teacher or administrator who works in an ACSI-accredited school must undergo a background investigation.
- **Regular updates**—Learning is for a lifetime. That's why we require that all ACSI-certified teachers and administrators meet regular checks and balances. All teachers and administrators must apply for recertification every two to five years (the timing for recertification depends on the type of certification they have received). To successfully reapply, they must meet specific requirements for professional development and biblical studies as well as meet the Christian-philosophy-of-education requirement if not already completed.

It's hard work to evaluate people's transcripts and backgrounds, but the results are worth it. The men and women who work in the ACSI Certification Department are dedicated to assisting educators and schools in making sure academic and spiritual excellence is attained through appropriate credentialing. "I am regularly impressed by the quality of the men and women who work in today's Christian schools," says Merry. "They're strong educators and leaders. They have the academic qualifications. They've done their homework, and they've attained the high standards of teacher or administrator certification."

Still, there's only one way parents can make sure that Christian teachers are right for their kids: "The best thing is for parents to go to the school where they're thinking about sending their children," says Merry. "That way, they can observe the teachers in their classrooms, and they can sit down and visit with the administrators. If they do that, I think they will be as impressed as I am with the quality of people we have."

A PASSION FOR THE PROFESSION

Does it seem that I care deeply about the men and women who work most closely with your children day after day in Christian schools? If so, that's because I myself am a walking testimony to the ways Christian teachers and administrators can change students' lives. Throughout my life, God has used caring Christian teachers to make an impact on my life. And through these experiences, I discovered my own life's calling in education. I vividly remember the night when I realized God wanted me to be a Christian teacher.

I was with Bonnie, my then fiancée. The two of us were enjoying a snack in the snack bar of the student center at Cornerstone University. We were contemplating our futures when I said this to Bonnie: "Bon, I am good at math and science. How can I use these abilities to serve the Lord?"

Her answer was clear: "Why don't you become a math teacher in a Christian school and impact students for the Lord like your teachers impacted you?"

The lightbulb lit up in my brain that day, and I never looked back. Christian schooling has been my life calling ever since.

In 1982 I returned to Elkhart Christian Academy, the Christian school from which I graduated in 1978. I taught math and science while Bonnie taught music and physical education. For the first fourteen years of my education career, I worked as a teacher, a coach, and an administrator. During those years, our four children were born. When our children were ready for kindergarten, Bonnie and I knew what we would do. Each child began classes at Elkhart Christian Academy.

After those fourteen years of joyful and fulfilling service, I accepted the call to become the superintendent of Heritage Christian School in Indianapolis, the school where Dan Stroup is a Bible teacher. During my tenure there Heritage grew to become the largest private K–12 school in the state of Indiana, enrolling sixteen hundred students—a beautiful, world-class school with outstanding academic, athletic, and fine arts facilities. After Heritage, I served the Lord as the vice president for university relations at Indiana Wesleyan University until July 2009.

In August of 2009 I was given the opportunity to begin working for ACSI, where I can work with many schools in many countries to make sure that the precious jewel of Christian education remains strong and powerful.

Because of my personal experience as a Christian teacher, I can promise you this—teachers in Christian schools aren't doing it for the money. When Bonnie and I started, each of us was making something between $5,000 and $10,000. That was for the entire school year!

Today we live in a time when celebrities and professional athletes make ridiculous amounts of money. Meanwhile, some of the people who do the important work of teaching are unfortunately paid too little. Rest assured, however, that many of the men and women who work with your children every day in our schools are motivated primarily by a profound sense of calling and not by financial security as the world defines it. This is the work they want to do with their lives. And your children are the direct beneficiaries of this commitment.

A LIVING CURRICULUM

Sometimes I wonder what would have happened to me if I had attended a different kind of school when I was a high school student. Any answer would be mere speculation. But I am so thankful that my father and mother sent me to a school where the teachers not only taught me about academic subjects but also helped guide me in the deeper things of life.

Because I attended a Christian school, I can agree with students I meet today who say, "My teachers live out their faith every day and show me how I can do the same."

Sometimes when I think about Jesus, I wonder why He was such a successful and powerful teacher when He was on earth. Of course, His being the Son of God helped. But what else helped Him have such a powerful impact on His disciples?

I believe that a major part of Jesus' approach to teaching was that He was a living curriculum. Jesus could have stayed at the side of His heavenly Father and communicated to the human race through lightning bolts or messages in the clouds. But that's not what He did. Through the miracle of the Incarnation, Jesus became a member of the human race. And as He walked with the disciples, ate with them, and worked alongside them, He taught them what being a God follower was all about (John 1:1, 14).

I believe that it was this living curriculum—expressed through the daily contact Jesus had with His disciples—that transformed the disciples' lives and consequently changed our world. Transformational teaching occurs in the context of relationships. Meaningful change happens life-on-life.

If you want your children to experience similar transformation in their lives, then entrust their education to caring and competent educators who share the same values you have. Teachers often spend more time in meaningful interaction with children than parents themselves do. Don't you want the teachers who will have an impact on your children's lives to be the kind of men and women described in this chapter?

Notes

1. View a YouTube video about Dan Stroup here: www.youtube.com/watch?v=gp6s3CIV4KQ.

2. To find out more about Dan Stroup's class, visit www.bibleisfun.com.

3. To learn more about the accreditation process ACSI and its member schools use to evaluate teachers and administrators, please select the *Accreditation* link under the Schools tab on the ACSI home page (www.acsi.org).

AN INVESTMENT
THAT KEEPS ON GIVING

I don't often quote Bart Simpson, the eternally obnoxious son featured in TV's popular animated series *The Simpsons*. But I can't help mentioning Bart's famous and sassy predinner prayer: "Dear God, we paid for this stuff ourselves, so thanks for nothing."

After giving you a moment to collect yourself, I want to tell you why I think Bart's prayer is a sad but truthful commentary on the cognitive dissonance that many twenty-first-century Christians experience.

When you read the words of Jesus, particularly His teaching in the Sermon on the Mount (Matthew 5–7), you can almost hear Him telling His followers not to base their lives on the things of this world. Jesus told His disciples how to pray, instructing them to make this request to God: "Give us today our daily bread" (Matthew 6:11). But I don't know many believers who take this verse literally. A few verses later, you can see the cure Jesus gives for worldly care:

> Do not store up for yourselves treasures on earth, where moth and rust destroy, and where thieves break in and steal. But store up for yourselves treasures in heaven, where moth and rust do not destroy,

and where thieves do not break in and steal. For where your treasure is, there your heart will be also. (6:19–21)

Unfortunately, I know many Christians who seem to follow the words of Bart Simpson more than the words of Jesus. Sometimes our worries about money prevent us from living the way we should.

Anyone can see these worries on the faces of parents when they try to determine whether to spend the money required to send their children to a Christian school. Some of these parents are facing real financial struggles—as many people have been in recent years. Other parents seem to have all the money they need, but they still aren't sure if they want to part with any of it to pay for a Christian school when they could send their children to public schools, which are paid for by taxpayer dollars.

I understand these concerns. They are legitimate, and they are a part of the process every parent goes through when choosing Christian education.

I also realize that I am not the most unbiased source on the value of Christian schooling. I firmly believe that a Christian school education is one of the very best investments Christian parents can make to help their children choose to become sold-out Christ followers. I am a product of Christian schools. My wife and I sent our kids to Christian schools. And I have worked in Christian schooling, both K–12 and postsecondary, throughout my professional career. That's why I am not going to try to convince you to accept my position. Instead, in this chapter, I am going to introduce you to parents just like you who share the same financial struggles you have. I think you will find their insights helpful.

In chapter 1 of this book, I argued that God entrusts His children to parents, at least for a while, and that during these years parents, as God's stewards, are to care for those children. In this chapter, we will look at the dollars-and-cents implications of this stewardship.

A FATHER'S STORY: MONEY FOR OUR MIRACLE CHILD

I know many parents who feel that their children are amazing miracles from God, but this realization is especially true of the Broas family, who after many long years of unsuccessfully trying to have a child nearly lost both the son and the mother during a difficult birth.

Both parents would have liked to tell this story together, but mother Minnie died after a battle with cancer in 2008, so father Dan will provide the details.

> Minnie and I grew up in churches that didn't teach us about having a personal relationship with Jesus. Minnie came to know Jesus, thanks to people she worked with at Young Life, and she introduced me to Jesus too. When we were married and started talking about having children, we both knew that Christ needed to be at the center of their education.
>
> After four years of trying, we had been unable to have children. It was only when we decided to adopt a child that the Lord gave us a big surprise. Minnie was pregnant, so instead of adopting we would have our own child.
>
> But Minnie's pregnancy was very difficult, and Daniel was born premature. There were times during the pregnancy and delivery that I feared I would lose both of them. But God had other plans. Daniel was born safe and sound, and his mother recovered after spending two weeks in intensive care.
>
> Maybe every parent feels that a new child is a miracle baby, but for us that feeling was especially strong. We knew Daniel was a special

gift from the Lord, and we truly believed that God had a special purpose for him. Minnie and I felt that we needed to prepare him for that purpose. That's why we decided to send him to a Christian school. We felt this would give him a solid foundation that would equip him for the purposes the Lord had for him.

This was not an easy decision, because we were not in a strong financial position. I was serving as a technical sergeant in the Air Force, so I was not earning very much. But we knew we had to do this. In our hearts we knew it was an investment in the future, so Minnie started working to help out financially. Still, there were times when we had to cut things from our budget to pay for Daniel's schooling. When he was in the fourth grade, we decided we really needed to cut down on a bunch of stuff, including our cell phones. We would do whatever it took to send Daniel to a Christian school, because that was one of our top priorities.

Daniel excelled as a student, a leader, and a follower of Jesus. There were times when other schools approached us about having Daniel participate in their [International] Baccalaureate programs for top students. But we knew he was receiving an excellent education at the Christian school, along with the Christian teaching and influence we felt was essential for his future. We continued to make the sacrifices necessary to make this happen.

Before her death, Minnie was able to see the fruits of our investment in Daniel. He has a really deep relationship with the Lord. He is a real leader in school and has served as student body president many years. He leads the students in praise and worship, and he's leading the kids in making positive changes for their lives and for the school.

Daniel will graduate this June, and he has already earned a number of college credits while attending high school. He is most interested in civil engineering and wants to work in developing countries to help people build roads, bring in better water to drink, and help them with other infrastructure needs. That's where the Lord is leading him. That's the type of ministry he wants to do.

Looking back on Daniel's first eighteen years, I am so thankful that Minnie and I made the commitment to invest in sending him to a Christian school. It has been a joy to see him grow stronger in the Lord. I don't think he would be the man he is right now if he had gone to public schools.

Proverbs tells parents to "train a child in the way he should go, and when he is old he will not turn from it" (Proverbs 22:6). That's what we have tried to do as parents. Dan is a gift from the Lord. We wanted him to have a strong foundation for the rest of his life, and now I feel he is really prepared for the future.

A BUSINESS PROFESSOR'S STORY: IT'S ALL ABOUT ROI

Dan and Minnie's story about Daniel shows how a typical mother and father determined what kind of education their son needed. But what happens when the father of the house has a PhD in human resource management from Rutgers, a master's degree in industrial and labor relations from Cornell, and a bachelor's degree in economics?

Michael Zigarelli is an associate professor of management at Messiah College in Grantham, Pennsylvania, and the former dean of the Regent University School of Business. His research in the fields of management, practical theology, law, and ethics has appeared in a number of scholarly journals and magazines, and he is the author (or coauthor) of ten books, including *The Minister's MBA* (Nashville, TN: B&H Publishing Group, 2006) and *Management by Proverbs* (Chicago, IL: Moody, 1999).

Michael and his wife, Tara, approached the Christian schooling question the same way many other parents do, except that Michael added a layer of economic analysis to the equation. Here's his story of why he and his wife chose a Christian school for their children:

> As a business school professor, I tend to think in terms of return on investment, or ROI. So when Tara and I considered shifting our four elementary-age kids from public school to Christian school, I asked these questions:
> - What's the return on investing in a Christian school education?
> - What's the real value of a Christian-based education?
> - Should we spend money today that we could earmark for college?
> - Is a Christian school really worth the price tag?
>
> In our case the price tag was daunting. When we did the math, we realized we were making a commitment for a six-figure expense through twelfth grade—about the price of a couple of college educations ... or the principal on our mortgage.
>
> Most business professors don't get paid as much as the executives we teach, so I admit that it was tempting at that point to stay with the status quo, especially since the public schools in our district were pretty decent. Compared to our local Christian school, there wasn't a huge gap in SAT scores or college entrance rates. So why not just save the money and rely on home and church for values education?
>
> Frankly, we concluded, values education through home and church would simply not be enough for us. Kids, like adults, often adopt the values of their peers and teachers, and we saw signs that this was already starting to happen. We were diligently pouring ourselves into our kids' lives at home, training them up in faith and virtue to the best of our ability. But seven hours a day, five days a week, they were being subtly reeducated, marinated in a secular worldview that was competing for their precious, malleable minds.

Like so many parents, Tara and I want our kids to be in a safe, nurturing, small-class, academically challenging environment. That's certainly a big part of the ROI for Christian education. But the other bottom line in Christian schools is character development, renewing children's minds so that they're God-centered rather than self-centered when making choices.

Someday—someday too soon!—our four kids will be making those choices without consulting us. Tara and I want to help them to choose wisely throughout their lives by shaping their hearts today to love God. It's the most important responsibility that God has entrusted to us, so we can use all the help we can get, seven hours a day, five days a week.

That's why we selected a local Christian school—Hershey Christian—for our kids. It's a school with caring and experienced teachers, a school with terrific facilities, a school with small classes and a big commitment to academic excellence, and most of all, a school that nurtures our kids' spiritual lives without being legalistic about it. Though the financial pressure is sometimes great, the return on that investment—well-educated kids who genuinely love God and neighbor—is far greater.

NEW SHOES OR TUITION?

After sharing these stories from parents, I also want to share a story about a student who performed his own analysis of the return on investment that Christian schooling could bring. Sometimes we choose to make an investment before we can envision the full return.

Most parents know that the typical Christian school receives a fourth or more of its annual income from donations that are provided by generous individuals, churches, and other institutions. The tuition received from parents simply isn't enough to cover all the costs. That's why schools often have capital campaigns to raise money for new programs or facilities.

Most of the time, it is adults who donate to Christian schools, but I want to introduce you to a young man who shows us adults how things should be done. The young man I heard about (he wanted to remain anonymous) was a student at Tree of Life Christian School–Northridge, which serves an ethnically and economically diverse population in Columbus, Ohio.

Tree of Life Superintendent Todd Marrah describes the surprising donation he received during one recent capital campaign:

> As a school administrator, I have the opportunity to get to know many parents and area pastors. A pastor of one of our city's largest African American churches invited me to speak at his church's men's conference. During my presentation, I briefly mentioned our school's capital campaign. At the end of the conference, one of our high school students who attended the men's conference told me that the Lord had told him to give $100 to our campaign. Later, the boy's mother e-mailed me to let me know that her son had been saving that money to buy a pair of basketball shoes but had felt like the Lord wanted him to give it to the school. After he donated his $100 to the school, another member of his church gave him not one pair but two pairs of the new basketball shoes he had wanted (one pair for practice and the other for games). But that's not all.
>
> Soon the family was in financial trouble. Both parents lost their jobs and were forced to consider withdrawing their four children from Tree of Life. But then a miracle happened! When other parents in the school and the family's church heard about the family's financial distress, they wrote a $10,000 check to cover all of the year's remaining tuition. So the student's $100 donation was multiplied a hundredfold. These are the kinds of money miracles I think we would see more often if we relied more on God's provision for our needs.

AN IMPORTANT STUDY ON CHRISTIAN SCHOOL OUTCOMES

A father's investment in his miracle child, a business professor's thoughts on the ROI of his four children's education costs, and a school superintendent's story about a student willing to sacrifice a pair of basketball shoes in order to donate to his school's capital campaign … but you may still be wondering whether Christian schooling is worth all of this. Maybe a quick look at some results of a 2011 study will provoke thought and strengthen my case for Christian schooling. The Cardus Education Survey is a research project that was developed to answer some basic questions about the effectiveness of Christian school education in North America. Ray Pennings, a senior fellow with Cardus[1] and the person who headed the project, reveals some of this survey's findings in an op-ed piece for a Center for Public Justice publication:

> Compared to their public school, Catholic school, and non-religious private school peers, Protestant Christian school graduates have been found to be uniquely compliant, generous, outwardly focused individuals who stabilize their communities by their uncommon commitment to their families, their churches, and larger society. This study found that graduates of Christian schools donate money significantly more than graduates of other schools, despite having a lower household income than graduates of other private schools. Similarly, graduates of Christian schools are more generous with their time, participating in far more relief and development service trips than their peers. (Pennings 2011)

Pennings refers to the products of Christian schools as " 'salt of the earth' citizens," people who provide stability for their communities and churches, stating that the Cardus study demonstrates the positive impact of Christian school graduates on society (2011). It's good to know that vital and credible research is being conducted on the culture-shaping role of Christian schooling, even though the full extent of Christian school graduates' contributions to families, churches, communities, and even the world will never be exhaustively quantified by any study or researcher.

THE CURE FOR AFFLUENZA

Superintendent Marrah's story illustrates the real problem with the Bart Simpson prayer I quoted to open this chapter. God wants all of us to realize that everything we have—including "our" children and "our" money—is really *His*. What He wants us to do is live as good and faithful stewards of the many great gifts He has showered on us.

Unfortunately, not all believers actually live this way. In fact, I think many of us actually behave as materialists who are suffering from a bad case of what has been termed *affluenza*. Let me explain what I mean.

Many years ago, after Bonnie and I graduated from college, we accepted our first teaching jobs. My first contract was for $9,600, and Bonnie's first contract was for $5,600. Today's Christian teachers don't survive on such meager salaries, but they often still earn much less than their public school counterparts, to say nothing of entertainers or professional athletes who make millions every year.

As I look at America, I see that we live in an affluent, sports-crazed, entertainment-driven, success-minded, and secular culture that has embraced fatally misplaced priorities. Unfortunately, many churches and Christian families appear to be buying into this culture.

The economic recession of recent years has confronted us with the flaws of the old buy-now-pay-later approach to life. But many continue to suffer the consequences of massive debt, decreasing house values, and diminishing accounts for our children's education and our retirement.

I have heard people cite the current economic situation as the reason they are not sending their children to Christian schools. But I wonder if the current situation doesn't instead show us the even more urgent need to make sure our children receive the Christian foundation they need to help lead us out of this mess.

Our children learn not only in classrooms; they learn also by watching the adults in their lives make decisions about what those adults' priorities are. In some cases, children hear their parents say that the parents' top priority is God's kingdom and God's rule in the family's lives (Matthew 6:33), but that commitment isn't always evident in the way the parents spend their money.

All private schools struggle with the tension that exists between what to charge parents for tuition and how much to pay teachers in salary and benefits, not to mention how to pay for expenses like extracurricular programs, technology, and costs related to new construction, renovation, maintenance, and upkeep of buildings and grounds.

And the costs of Christian schooling actually start years before your children enter the classroom. Starting and maintaining a quality, Christ-centered Christian school begins when land is acquired and a school is first built. At this time, there are no students paying tuition. Instead there is a group of caring and concerned Christian adults who want the best for their children and will do whatever is needed to make that happen.

Parents who are concerned about tuition costs don't realize that for some Christian schools, there are actually two "checks" written every month. The first is the check parents write for tuition. The second is an invisible check many teachers write in the form of the difference between their salary and the bigger salary that they could be receiving in the public sector. This is their financial investment in their students' futures.

WHICH VALUES WILL RULE US?

I believe that times of crisis present times of opportunity. It has even been said that a crisis is a terrible thing to waste!

The current economic uncertainties of our world have led many people to ask the question, What truly matters in life? That's a good thing. But it's how we answer this question that is most important.

I am convinced that one of the biggest obstacles our children face in developing a closer walk with God is materialism. We sometimes resemble the rich young man who came to Jesus and asked what was necessary to be saved. All went well until Jesus commanded the man to sell all he owned, give the proceeds to the poor, and follow Jesus. The Bible says, "When the young man heard this, he went away sad, because he had great wealth" (Matthew 19:22).

In American culture, materialism is so pervasive that we can now see, in young people as well as in adults, the symptoms of a spiritual disease called affluenza. The main symptoms of affluenza are apathy and dissatisfaction. Enough is never enough.

The best way to battle affluenza in our personal lives and in our nation is to strive to keep our priorities straight. This is often a battle in Christian homes, schools, and churches because we are daily sucking on the fumes of a secular culture. Materialism puts self and material wealth on the throne of our lives in place of God. The only way to correct this error is to allow God to be on the throne of our lives.

And the best way to help our children battle affluenza is to first conquer it in our own lives. Only then can we encourage them to give of themselves and their material resources for the benefit of others.

Finally, one of the best ways to be good stewards of the amazing gifts God has given us, including our children and our financial resources, is to devote both to God's work in the world. I have a feeling that if you truly seek His will for all He has entrusted to your care, the costs of Christian school tuition may begin to seem like a smart investment in the future, both for your children and for the world.

Note

1. Cardus is a think tank that conducts research on education and culture, among other key areas. To learn more about this organization, visit www.cardus.ca.

OUR HOPE FOR THE FUTURE

Thank you for joining me in this look at the heart, soul, and mind of Christian schools around the world. As this book comes to a close, I want to share with you perhaps the most important characteristic of Christian schools and the one thing that unites all the wonderful men and women who work in them as faculty, staff, and administration members.

I believe that Christian schools are our hope for the future! Let me tell you two stories that will show you exactly what I mean.

COURAGE AND CHARACTER ON 9/11

We can all probably remember exactly where we were when we heard the awful news about the attacks on America on September 11, 2001. I was in my office at Heritage Christian School when one of our normally cheerful office staff members threw open my door and rushed in, tears streaming down her face.

At the same moment, a thirty-two-year-old man named Todd Beamer was a passenger on United Airlines Flight 93, which was on its way from Newark, New Jersey, to San Francisco, California. As the plane passed over Ohio, it made a sudden turn toward the southeast. Were the plane's hijackers taking this flight toward New

York or Washington, where they could fly it into a skyscraper or a national monument?

The passengers on the plane weren't sure what the hijackers were intending. But Todd took the lead, and he and the other passengers decided they would not sit back and do nothing. They organized themselves into a tactical strike force that confronted the terrorists. And while the outcome of their efforts was a tragedy for all on board, their actions prevented the plane from becoming yet another terrorist tool, like the planes that flew into the World Trade Center towers and the Pentagon, to kill thousands of people. Instead the plane crashed into the ground near Shanksville, Pennsylvania, far away from big cities or large populations.

Just before Todd and his fellow passengers confronted the hijackers, Todd had been on a phone call with a GTE supervisor, the person who heard his last words: "Are you guys ready? Okay. Let's roll" (Beamer 2002, 214).

The story of this now-famous hero, including some of Todd's experiences as a student at the ACSI member school Wheaton Academy, is told in the bestselling book *Let's Roll: Ordinary People, Extraordinary Courage*, which was authored by Todd's wife, Lisa. In the book, Lisa mentions friendships and leadership roles that Todd experienced at Wheaton Academy, an outstanding Christian school that was founded in 1853 by the same people who would later found Wheaton College.

Now, can I make the claim that Wheaton Academy (named Wheaton Christian High School when Todd attended) gave Todd Beamer the courage to do what he did that day? No. But I am convinced that the school's emphasis on character and courage, as well as the quality relationships he developed at the school, played a powerful role in making Todd into the kind of man he was. I am also convinced that

Christian schools worldwide are preparing thousands of young men and women for the important roles they courageously will play in life to the glory of God.

A HIGHER GOAL

The second story deals with faith and football. Football is a big deal for millions of Americans, perhaps nowhere more so than in Texas. And at Faith Christian School in Grapevine, Texas, football is a very big deal indeed. But as the following story, originally written by sportswriter Rick Reilly (2008), shows, the students and coaches at Faith Christian placed their love for God above their love of winning football games in a powerful way:

> Grapevine, Texas—one of *Money Magazine*'s top 100 "best places to live" in 2007—is almost 90% white, has a $90,000 median family income, and award-winning schools like Faith Christian School. Like most towns in Texas, Grapevine takes its high school football seriously. Faith's football team, for example, has seventy players, eleven coaches, the latest equipment, and hordes of involved parents. In November 2008, the Faith Lions were 7–2 going into the game with the Gainesville State Tornados.
>
> Gainesville State, on the other hand, headed into the game 0–8, having scored only two touchdowns all year. Gainesville's fourteen players wore seven-year-old pads and dilapidated helmets and were escorted by twelve security guards who took off the players' handcuffs before the game. Gainesville State, a maximum security prison north of Dallas, gets its students by court order. Many Tornados have convictions for drugs, assaults, and robberies. Many of their families have disowned them. They play every game on the road.
>
> Before the game, Faith's head coach Kris Hogan had an idea. What if, just for one night, half of the Faith fans cheered for the kids on the opposing team? "Here is the message I want you to send," Hogan

wrote in an email to Faith's faithful. "You are just as valuable as any other person on Planet Earth." The Faith fans agreed.

When the Gainesville Tornados took the field, they crashed through a banner made by Faith fans that read "Go Tornados!" The Gainesville players were surprised to find themselves running through a forty-foot spirit line made up of cheering fans. From their benches at the side of the field, the Gainesville team heard two hundred fans on the bleachers behind them, cheering for them by name, led by real cheerleaders (Hogan had recruited the JV squad to cheer for the opposing team). "I thought maybe they were confused," said Alex, a Gainesville lineman. Another lineman, Gerald, said: "We can tell people are a little afraid of us when we come to the games.... But these people, they were yellin' for us! By our names!" Gainesville's quarterback and middle linebacker Isaiah shook his head in disbelief. "I never thought I'd hear people cheering for us to hit their kids.... But they wanted us to!"

At the end of the game (Faith won, 33–14), the losing team practically danced off the field with their fingers pointing #1 in the air. They gave Gainesville's head coach Mark Williams what ESPN sportswriter Rick Reilly described as the first Gatorade bath in history for a 0–9 coach. When the teams gathered in the middle of the field to pray, Isaiah surprised everybody by asking to lead. ("We had no idea what the kid was going to say," remembers Coach Hogan.) This was Isaiah's prayer: "Lord, I don't know how this happened, so I don't know how to say thank You, but I never would've known there was so many people in the world that cared about us."

As guards escorted the Tornados back to their bus, each player received a bag filled with burgers, fries, candy, a Bible, and an encouraging letter from a Faith player. Before he stepped onto the bus, Williams turned and grabbed Hogan hard by the shoulders: "You'll never know what your people did for these kids tonight.

You'll never, ever know." The Gainesville players crowded onto one side of the bus, peering out the windows at an unbelievable sight—people they had never met before smiling at them, waving goodbye, as the bus drove into the night.

It was, in Reilly's words, "rivers running uphill and cats petting dogs"—or, as another Isaiah put it:

The wolf shall live with the lamb, the leopard shall lie down with the kid,

the calf and the lion and the fatling together,

and a little child shall lead them (Isa. 11:6 [NRSV]). (Dean 2010, 85–87; ellipses in original)

Don't you wish that all high school football players (and all the players' parents) could learn from a teacher like Coach Hogan and practice the coach's message: "You are just as valuable as any other person on Planet Earth" (Dean 2010, 86)?

The story above was featured in Kenda Creasy Dean's 2010 book titled *Almost Christian: What the Faith of Our Teenagers Is Telling the American Church*. Much of this book conveys bad news (17). The book is based on extensive studies that reveal how many churches and youth groups are failing to disciple their children to grow into solid, mature Christians.

The author of *Almost Christian* chose this story about Faith Christian School because that football game is a powerful example of Christian instruction that worked. And if you were to visit as many Christian schools as I have, I am sure you could find many equally powerful stories about Christian students whose lives are being transformed by the teachers and coaches who work with them. These coaches understand the power of athletics as a tool to prepare devoted followers of Jesus Christ, and life lessons similar to the one learned by those Faith students will long outlive memories of games won or lost.

A GREAT NEED

Stories like these about Todd Beamer and the students at Faith Christian give me hope because they reveal that Christian schools are preparing young men and women for whatever will confront them in their lives and their world.

The world is growing bigger and more complex every day. The challenges that adults like you and me have faced in the past will be eclipsed by the issues that our kids will be forced to confront when they become old enough to run the world on their own.

If there is anything we need in the future, it is a group of young leaders who hold tightly to the biblical foundations of their faith while opening their arms to serve the world around them, as God would have them do.

I believe that Christian schools are an essential ingredient in helping our children meet the challenges they will face. Parents like us mean well, but our kids need additional teachers and mentors to guide them into a deeper, more meaningful faith. Churches—along with youth groups and parachurch organizations—also mean well, and they achieve much. But children need more than a weekly or twice-weekly connection to Christian teaching. And in Christian schools, children receive that kind of teaching five days a week, regardless of whether they are studying Bible, English, or history.

SEEK WHAT'S BEST

You know your kids best, and God has entrusted you—not me—to make the all-important decisions about how you will instruct them as they grow into adulthood.

My goal in writing this book was to make the strong case for Christian schooling, and I have given it my best shot.

I pray that as you seek what's best for your children's education and future, you will consider a Christian school. And I hope that you will go beyond considering to actually visiting a school near you so you can see for yourself its people and programs.

As parents, we are stewards of a sacred trust, and God has placed His children into our care for only a short time. May we faithfully carry out that trust in a way that glorifies Him and prepares our children for both this life and the life to come.

REFERENCES

Averill, Mike. 2010. Happy Hands School enjoys new building. *Tulsa World*, September 14. http://www.tulsaworld.com/news/article.asp x?subjectid=11&articleid=20100914_11_A9_ULNSib470472.

Beamer, Lisa. 2002. *Let's roll: Ordinary people, extraordinary courage.* With Ken Abraham. Carol Stream, IL: Tyndale.

Bridges, Jerry. 1988. *Trusting God even when life hurts.* Colorado Springs, CO: NavPress.

Colson, Chuck. 2009. Evangelicalism in America: Waxing or waning? BreakPoint Commentaries. http://www.breakpoint.org/ commentaries/1870-evangelicalism-in-america.

Dean, Kenda Creasy. 2010. *Almost Christian: What the faith of our teenagers is telling the American Church.* New York: Oxford University Press.

Hendricks, Howard G., and William D. Hendricks. 1991. *Living by the book.* Chicago, IL: Moody.

Pennings, Ray. 2011. Are Christian school graduates world-changers? *Capital Commentary*, May 20. http://www.capitalcommentary.org/ religious-education/are-christian-school-graduates-world-changers.

Reilly, Rick. 2008. There are some games when cheering for the other side feels better than winning. *ESPN: The Magazine*, December 23. http://sports.espn.go.com/espnmag/story?section= magazine&id=3789373. Cited in Dean 2010.

Schultz, Glen. 1998. *Kingdom education: God's plan for educating future generations.* 2nd ed. Nashville, TN: LifeWay.

Smith, Dwayne K. 2009. *The Christian athlete: Honoring God through sports.* Mustang, OK: Tate.

Swan, Scott. 2009. Local teacher sends annual greetings to every former student. *Eyewitness News*, November 4. www.wthr.com/Global/story.asp?S=11443986.

Tucker, Mike. 2010. Pen man. *AARP Bulletin*, January–February, 8.

Wolterstorff, Nicholas P. 2002. *Educating for life: Reflections on Christian teaching and learning.* Ed. Gloria Goris Stronks and Clarence W. Joldersma. Grand Rapids, MI: Baker Academic.